the self-care cookbook

the self-care cookbook

Easy Healing Plant-Based Recipes

Gemma Ogston

Clarkson Potter/Publishers
NEW YORK

Published in the United States by Clarkson Potter/Publishers, an imprint of Random House, a division of Penguin Random House LLC, New York.

clarksonpotter.com

CLARKSON POTTER is a trademark and POTTER with colophon is a registered trademark of Penguin Random House LLC.

First published in Great Britain by Vermilion in 2019.

Library of Congress Cataloging-in-Publication Data
Names: Ogston, Gemma, author. | Bellorini, James, photographer.
Title: The self-care cookbook : easy healing plant-based recipes / Gemma Ogston.
Description: New York : Clarkson Potter, [2020] | Photographs by James Bellorini. |
Identifiers: LCCN 2019058627 (print) | LCCN 2019058628 (ebook) | ISBN 9780593139462 (hardcover) | ISBN 9780593139479 (ebook)
Subjects: LCSH: Vegetarian cooking. | Cooking (Natural foods) | LCGFT: Cookbooks.
Classification: LCC TX837 .O37 2020 (print) | LCC TX837 (ebook) | DDC 641.5/636—dc23
LC record available at https://lccn.loc.gov/2019058627
LC ebook record available at https://lccn.loc.gov/2019058628

ISBN 978-0-593-13946-2

Ebook ISBN 978-0-593-13947-9

Proprietary ISBN 978-0-525-61705-1

Cover photographs by Gemma Ogston

Photographs on pages 7, 71, and 190 © 2019 by James Bellorini

Printed in the United States of America

10 9 8 7 6 5 4 3 2 1

contents

Life is busy. These days, it can often seem as though we all have a never-ending list of things we should have done yesterday, and it's easy to feel overwhelmed and a little lost at times. If this has been going on for a while, it can even leave us experiencing low moods or poor sleep and we can be more susceptible to illnesses. When we're feeling like this, it's more important than ever that we look after ourselves. Through taking some proper time to nourish our bodies and minds, we can restore our energies and regain balance.

The Self-Care Cookbook is a combination of wholesome plant-based recipes for self-care, moments of quiet reflection, and masses of practical steps you can take to show yourself the love and attention you deserve. It's divided into the key stages of your self-care journey: Restore, Rebalance, Reflect, and Renew— with a special chapter on TLC, for when you need to show yourself some extra kindness.

It's simple: when we make an effort to eat more healthily and take proper time to rest, recharge, and do more of the things we enjoy, we feel better and happier. And this means we're stronger and more able to deal with whatever life sends our way.

Please don't see taking a break in order to restore and recover as a sign of weakness or an indulgence. It is, in fact, one of the truest signs of strength and wisdom. Being able to listen to how you are really feeling and identifying when you need to take a step back is intuitive and powerful. It is not selfish or lazy.

My own journey to eating a much healthier diet began about eight years ago, when I was struggling to have a baby. We had suffered many miscarriages and so I started to look at how my diet may be impacting not only my physical health but also my mental health and general mood. After switching to mainly plant-based meals, I quickly saw improvements and, as

a family, we stopped eating meat five years ago. A combination of reasons led us to becoming vegetarian, including animal welfare, environmental issues, health, and money. Soon after, I also gave up dairy, and I found I no longer experienced terrible coughs and chest infections. For me, my health, energy levels, and mood all improved dramatically when eating a mainly whole food, plant-based diet. But, of course, life is all about balance, and sometimes self-care means cutting yourself an extra slice of cake. . . .

I have studied plant-based nutrition and so all the meals I create for my family and for Gem's Wholesome Kitchen are well balanced, using plants, whole grains, and healthy fats. Within each section of this book are also recipes aimed at helping you with whatever specific challenges you are currently experiencing—perhaps you are struggling to sleep or are facing big changes in your life, or maybe you are recovering from an illness. The ingredients are carefully chosen to ease anxiety, help you rest better, lift your mood, or give you energy while nourishing and caring for you. I believe that self-care recipes are also about enjoying the process of preparing the recipes and eating them—making meals look bright and cheerful and putting love into cooking them is an act of self-care in itself. I love to cook with an abundance of wonderful veggies, as just seeing all the bright and happy colors lifts my mood before I have even started!

It's not all about food, though; practical acts of self-care are so important for good physical and mental health, and they can help us feel more in control of our well-being. Each chapter of this book contains ideas for getting back in tune with our needs—from getting more nature into our lives, connecting with friends, family, and our local community, and appreciating the little things to the importance of creativity and easy ways to bring more joy into our day-to-day.

The Self-Care Cookbook is a holistic approach to self-care. I hope it will nourish your body and mind and restore you back to your true self.

In my pantry

If you have a well-stocked pantry, you will always be able to put together a tasty meal in no time. I love to have lots of spices and herbs on hand, as they add instant flavor and excitement to dishes. Nearly all these ingredients can be bought at your usual supermarket, but I recommend seeking out the few more unusual ones from your local health food shop or Asian supermarket, too, as they really will take your cooking to the next level with the minimum of effort.

Cans and jars

Canned **legumes** are great for using in stews and salads and for making quick dips. They are an easy way to add protein, too. I always make sure I have **chickpeas, kidney beans,** and **lima beans.**

Cans of **tomatoes** are a go-to staple, as is **coconut milk** (for soups and curries). I also keep premade, good-quality vegan **pesto** for quick pasta dishes.

Dried grains and legumes

Perfect for Buddha bowls, to bulk up salads, as a quick side, or to boost the nutritional content of any meal. My favorites are **red and green lentils, quinoa, brown rice** and **Arborio or other risotto rice,** and **pearl barley. Bulgur wheat** is also great added to soups. **Rolled oats** are a must for overnight oats, crumble toppings, and porridge, so I always have lots of these.

Pasta and noodles

Because we all need pasta in our lives! If you are gluten-free, there are some great choices out there these days. Keep a range of **whole wheat pasta shapes, lasagne,** and **spaghetti,** as well as **buckwheat noodles** and **rice noodles** for ramen and stir-fries.

Flour

Keep a few different flours for baking and making pastry. I usually have jars of **whole wheat flour, chickpea flour,** and **gluten-free flour.**

Natural sweeteners

I prefer to cook with **unrefined natural sweeteners** such as **maple syrup, coconut sugar, honey,** and **raw cane sugar.** I also use **brown sugar.**

Oils

I use **olive oil** in most of my cooking and for making salad dressings. I also use coconut oil in sweet dishes and some savory dishes, such as curries. It's good to have a small bottle of **sesame oil**, too, as this adds an extra layer of flavor when cooking Asian dishes.

Vinegars

Great for adding an extra tang to soups or stews. **Raw apple cider vinegar** is my go-to, as it's full of probiotics, which are great for gut health. **Balsamic vinegar** is also nice for quick salad dressings.

Plant-based milks

Have a good stock of your favorite plant-based milks for making sauces, drinks, and smoothies. I like **unsweetened oat** and **almond milks**. Also see page 17 for how to make your own nut milks.

Nuts, seeds, and dried fruits

I use these in a lot of my recipes as they are an easy way to get in extra nutrients—and nuts add protein, too. They are great for snacking on and add instant interest to salads and porridge. Keep a range of the following:

- Chia seeds
- Flax seeds
- Sesame seeds
- Pumpkin seeds
- Sunflower seeds
- Walnuts
- Almonds
- Brazil nuts
- Peanuts
- Cashews
- Pecans
- Nut butters—almond and peanut (make sure you look for palm oil–free versions)
- Raisins
- Dried apricots
- Dates
- Dried berries (such as cranberries and goji berries)

Flavor boosters

Definitely try to source these if you can, as they will add amazing extra flavor to your cooking—and a little goes a long way, so they will last for ages!

- **Tomato paste**—a cooking staple for enriching tomato dishes.
- **Tamari**—this is like a gluten-free version of soy sauce that adds a lovely rich flavor—try it in the mushrooms on toast on page 28.
- **Nutritional yeast**—a deactivated yeast, high in vitamin B_{12}. It has an almost cheesy taste, so try it in the pesto on page 18.
- **Liquid smoke**—this is an incredible ingredient made by burning wood and collecting the smoke, which then becomes a liquid as it cools. It is very strong and makes food taste as though it's been cooked on a barbecue! Try it in the Jackfruit Taco Party on page 64.
- **Dried seaweed and mushrooms**—these add instant depth of flavor and extra minerals to stocks and stews—try them in the ramen on page 40.

Herbs and spices

I LOVE herbs and spices and put them in almost all of my cooking. They make all the difference and I find their aromas really lift my mood. This is by no means an exhaustive list, but these are a great place to get started.

- Bay leaves
- Chile powder
- Cinnamon (ground and stick)
- Cloves
- Curry powder
- Freshly ground black pepper
- Garam masala
- Garlic powder
- Ground coriander
- Ground cumin
- Ground ginger
- Ground turmeric
- Mustard seeds
- Nutmeg
- Onion powder
- Sea salt
- Smoked paprika (hot and sweet)

Baking

As well as a range of flours, keep these in your pantry for when only something sweet or chocolate-y will do!

- Cacao powder
- Good-quality dark chocolate
- Coconut flakes and/or shredded coconut
- Baking powder
- Vanilla extract
- Almond extract

Freezer

- **Frozen fruit** is brilliant for dessert and smoothies when you can't buy fresh in season. They are usually cheaper, too—I keep **berries**, **mango**, **pineapple**, and **sliced bananas**.
- **Frozen peas**—these are a staple for easy sides or adding to stews. They are also a good source of plant protein.
- **Veggie stock**—batch-made and frozen. See page 18 for my recipe.

Superfood powders

I use these to power up my smoothies or overnight oats. Most supermarkets now have their own brand versions selling for a lot less than the bigger names in health food shops.

- **Maca**—great for boosting your mood and balancing hormones.
- **Spirulina**—a powerful antioxidant and a rich source of omega-3.
- **Cacao**—improves brain function and a great mood booster.
- **Pea or hemp protein**—a great, quick protein boost for smoothies.

A NOTE ON ORGANIC

It's definitely not essential to always buy organic, but if you'd like to shop with this in mind, it doesn't always need to cost a lot.

1. **Shop around**
   Supermarkets will often have their own range of organic ingredients. Look out for offers and get to know when they drop their prices toward the end of the day.

2. **Eat seasonally when you can**
   It will tend to work out cheaper and, as it's in line with the natural cycle of our planet, it also helps keep us more in tune with nature.

3. **Join a local CSA**
   You can find some great local community-supported agriculture (CSA) programs that offer really well priced organic boxes that are so much cheaper than bigger brands, and, of course, they help support your local community, too.

4. **Try to grow a few bits of your own!**
   Even just a few pots of herbs (see page 95) or a few tomatoes. It's so satisfying, and you will be pleased with your achievements.

5. **Check out your local farmers' markets**
   Especially at the end of the day when they normally try to reduce produce to get rid of it. You could walk away with some real bargains and also end up with a heap of veggies that will inspire you to cook some new and exciting dishes.

6. **Explore apps**
   There are great apps that let people and businesses share surplus food and connect neighbors to share any food that would otherwise go to waste. You can get some amazing organic produce on these for free or very cheap. Anything that reduces food waste is obviously great!

PANTRY CLEANSE

When your kitchen and cupboards are messy, your mind can feel like that, too! Organize your pantry and you will instantly feel more clear-headed and energized. Plus, it will save you scrabbling around at the back of the cupboard looking for that spice jar when you're in the middle of cooking.

1. ## A good old sort-out!
   Lay everything out on a table so you can have a proper look. Go through all those cans, packages of dried foods, and jars and check the expiration dates. If there are any items in date that you know you're just not going to use, take them to a food bank or community kitchen.

2. ## Clean all those shelves so they gleam!

3. ## Organize sections
   Arrange everything in a logical order—maybe a baking section, a spices and herbs section, and a shelf for all the grains, and such. This will make it easier when you are looking for ingredients and you will be able to spot if you are running low. You could even go to town here and make some labels!

4. ## Write a shopping list
   Once you've had a good old clearout, treat yourself to some delicious, wholesome foods to make your pantry look inviting and inspire you to cook! See pages 10–12 for my favorite pantry items.

5. ## Stock up on healthy snacks
   Make a treat box and fill it with healthy snacks so that when you're in a hurry you can grab something that's good for you. Buy decent chocolate with a high percentage of cocoa and not much sugar. It will boost your mood while giving your sweet tooth a hit. Win!

DITCH THE PLASTIC!

Plastic is a big issue these days and I love to shop in zero-waste stores. These are shops where you bring your own containers and fill them up with however much you want. They even sell cleaning products and cosmetics now, which are organic and are often cheaper, too, as they are not packed in expensive plastic. Reuse old jam jars or pick up some glass storage jars from a thrift shop or market. There is nothing more satisfying than perusing your pantry and seeing lots of different jars full of colorful foods.

Recipes for everyday well-being

With a few essential components in your fridge or freezer, you can add instant flavor to dishes, create meals without even having to leave the house, and know that you're doing yourself some nutritional good, too, as they will be free from additives and unwanted extras.

Easy-peasy nut milk

I have used almonds here, but cashews will give you an even creamier milk. I tend to soak the nuts overnight in water and then make the milk in the morning. Use leftover nut meal to make energy balls, add it to granola, or mix with cooked grains for a nutty salad. You will need a nut bag, a square of cheese cloth, or a fine sieve to strain the milk.

MAKES 1 QUART
Prep time: 5 minutes
(plus soaking the nuts overnight)

1 cup raw almonds
a pinch of sea salt
1 date or 1 tsp maple syrup (optional)

Place the nuts in a bowl and cover with water by about ¾ inch. Cover with a cloth and let sit for up to 2 days in the fridge. The nuts will plump up as they absorb the water. When the nuts are soaked, drain and rinse them in a colander under cool running water.

In a blender, pulse the nuts and 1 quart water to break up the nuts, then blend on high speed for 3 minutes. Add the salt and the date or maple syrup, if you like. Blend for another minute. Pour the milk through a nut bag, layer of muslin, or a fine sieve into a large bowl. Squeeze and press to release as much milk as possible. Store the nut milk in a lidded bottle or jar in the fridge for up to 3 days.

Cashew cheese spread

Perfect spread on toast or dolloped on a baked potato for a fuss-free dinner, this cheesy treat will keep for up to five days in an airtight container in the fridge. You will need a food processor or blender for this recipe.

MAKES 2 PORTIONS
Prep time: 5 minutes
(plus soaking the nuts for at least 2 hours)

1 cup raw cashews
2 tbsp nutritional yeast
juice of 1 lemon
½ tsp garlic powder
1 tsp sea salt, or to taste
a pinch of freshly ground black pepper,
  or to taste

Place the nuts in a bowl and cover with water by about ¾ inch. Cover with a cloth and let sit at room temperature for at least 2 hours, and ideally overnight. The nuts will plump up as they absorb the water. When the nuts are soaked, drain and rinse them in a colander under cool running water.

Put everything in a food processor or blender. Pulse to roughly break down the cashews. Scrape down the sides, add ¼ cup water, and blend again for about 2 minutes, until smooth and thick, with the consistency of hummus; add an extra splash of water if needed. Taste and add more lemon juice, salt, and pepper if necessary.

Veggie stock

I sometimes roast the veggies first, as it gives the stock a deeper flavor, but don't worry if you don't have time. Dried seaweed and mushrooms will add even more nutrients and minerals, as well as enriching the flavor, but leave these out if you prefer. Make a big batch and freeze in smaller containers for up to three months.

MAKES 2 QUARTS
Prep time: 5 minutes
Cooking time: 1¼–2 hours

1 small onion, quartered (no need to peel)
4 garlic cloves (no need to peel)
4 carrots, roughly chopped
4 celery stalks, roughly chopped
7 oz mushrooms, wiped clean
a glug of olive oil, if roasting the veggies
a few sprigs of fresh thyme
a few sprigs of fresh rosemary
a small handful of freshly chopped parsley
2 bay leaves
a handful of dried seaweed (optional)
a handful of dried mushrooms (optional)

To roast the veg, preheat the oven to 425°F. In a large roasting pan, toss the fresh veg in the olive oil, thyme, and rosemary. Roast for 45 minutes.

Put all the ingredients and 2 quarts water in a large pot. Bring to a boil, then lower the heat and simmer for 1¼ hours. Cool a little, then strain through a sieve.

Perfect pesto

Brilliant with pasta, of course, but also try it in a toasted sandwich, on top of a baked potato, or stir a spoonful into soups and stews. It will keep in an airtight jar in the fridge for up to two weeks. You will need a food processor, blender, or a mortar and pestle. To vary the flavor and nutrients, add some kale, swap pine nuts for walnuts, and/ or add a squeeze of lemon juice.

MAKES 1 SMALL JAR
Prep time: 10 minutes

4 cups basil leaves
1 cup plus 2 tbsp pine nuts
2 garlic cloves
2 tbsp nutritional yeast
3 tbsp extra-virgin olive oil
sea salt and freshly ground black pepper,
    to taste

Put the basil, pine nuts, garlic, and nutritional yeast in a food processor or blender and blitz to a thick paste, scraping the sides as you go. Add the olive oil and 3 to 4 tablespoons of water, one tablespoon at a time, and keep blending until smooth. Alternatively, pound the basil, pine nuts, and garlic in a mortar and pestle to make a thick paste, then mix in the olive oil and 3 to 4 tablespoons of water, a tablespoon at a time, until you achieve a loose consistency. Season with salt and freshly ground black pepper, to taste.

Gut-happy vinaigrette

This tasty dressing is so simple to make and is delicious with any green leaves or drizzled over raw veggies for an easy light meal. I always try to use raw apple cider vinegar in my dressings, as it is full of probiotics, which are great for the gut—but feel free to use any other vinegar you like if you'd like to add a different flavor. This recipe makes enough to fill a small jar, but you can double up the quantities; it will keep for up to two weeks in the fridge.

MAKES ¾ CUP PLUS 2 TBSP
Prep time: 5 minutes

3 tbsp raw apple cider vinegar
1 tbsp Dijon mustard
2 tsp honey
a pinch of sea salt
a pinch of freshly ground black pepper
½ cup olive oil

Put all the ingredients in a blender and blend for 30 seconds. That's it! Alternatively, you can whisk everything together in a small bowl, or shake it in a sealed jar until combined.

Gem's granola

A must for your pantry. Serve with plant-based milk and fruit, or sprinkle on top of desserts, salads, or overnight oats for extra crunch. Add more dried fruits, nuts, or seeds if you like—anything goes! It will keep in an airtight container for up to three weeks.

MAKES 4 CUPS
Prep time: 5 minutes
Cooking time: 20 minutes

2 tbsp coconut oil
2–3 tbsp maple syrup or honey
2¼ cups rolled oats
⅓ cup raw nuts (such as almonds, walnuts, or pecans)
⅔ cup coconut flakes
½ cup seeds (such as sunflower or pumpkin seeds)
1 tsp vanilla extract
1 tsp ground cinnamon
a large pinch of sea salt
1 cup dried fruit (such as apricots, cranberries, or raisins), chopped if large (optional)

Preheat the oven to 400°F. Line a baking sheet with parchment paper. In a small pan, melt the coconut oil with the maple syrup or honey on low heat. Remove from the heat. In a bowl, combine all the dry ingredients, except the dried fruit. Pour in the melted oil and mix well to coat. Spread in a thin, even layer on the lined baking sheet. Bake for 15 minutes, until lightly toasted. Leave to cool, then mix with the dried fruit and transfer to an airtight container.

Restore

Our busy lives and hectic schedules can often leave us running on empty. Now more than ever, it feels so important that we regularly set aside proper time to fully restore and recharge our energy levels. Often we find ourselves dealing with feelings of guilt if we plan to take some time out, as though we think we should be constantly chasing that to-do list, or maybe even that we think we don't deserve to stop and rest. But is there really anything more important than looking after our health? If we aren't looking after ourselves properly, how can we be expected to look after other people or perform to the best of our abilities? If we ignore our need to replenish our energies and carry on steaming ahead, illness or exhaustion can kick in, forcing us to take a break. It's obviously so much better if we can avoid reaching a breaking point in the first place. Remember that life isn't a competition about who can do more or who can operate on the least sleep.

This first chapter is all about retreating into yourself for a little while, slowing the pace down so that you can gather your energies together again. I've included sections on how to get more rest into your days, with ideas and recipes to calm the nerves and reduce anxiety, and to aid properly peaceful sleep. I've also shared an easy restorative mindfulness exercise, which you can even practice while you are preparing a delicious meal for yourself! The chapter closes with one of my favorite sections in the book—**Cozy**. Whether it's a sleep-in on the weekend or snuggling down into the sofa after a long day, I believe getting cozy is essential to our well-being. It should be a MUST in your self-care routine.

I hope by the end of this chapter, you will have started to feel a little calmer, recharged, and more in control. Bringing a sense of calm to how you go about your day, however chaotic life may feel at times, will leave you better able to cope with whatever you are facing.

rest

Good-quality rest—and enough of it—is vital for body and mind. Experiencing even low-level tiredness can lead to fluctuating moods and even forgetfulness. Although eight hours a night is often considered the Holy Grail when it comes to sleep, as a mum of two with a busy job, I know that this is not always possible for everyone. We also all need different amounts of sleep, so it's important to work out how much you need personally and then to try to aim for that whenever you can.

Don't worry if you're not getting as many hours each night as you think you should, but do take a look at ways you can introduce more moments of rest into your daily life and at improving the quality of the sleep that you do get. Maybe set aside one night a week to go to bed early or let yourself nap in the afternoon on the weekend if you're tired. Even just slowing things down a notch or two as you go about your day, allowing yourself to pause for a quiet moment or making the time to do absolutely nothing for a few hours every so often so you can relax and unwind, will help you feel all the more rested.

The recipes on the following pages contain my favorite restorative and calming ingredients to help boost melatonin production (which controls your body's internal clock) and to aid better sleep. These dishes can also help reduce anxiety so you can feel more relaxed and calmer throughout the day. Later in the chapter, I've shared a few of my tried-and-tested ways for achieving a truly restorative night's sleep.

If you are feeling unrested and exhausted, remember to be gentle with yourself. Know that it will pass eventually, and make sure not to overload your days or plan in too many activities that will drain your energies. We all go through patches of restlessness during our lives, but taking just a few small steps can help you gain back control.

Sometimes poor sleep can be due to something as simple as falling blood sugar levels during the night. Try one of these light snacks before bed and see if it makes any difference to how well you sleep.

- **A small bowl of porridge**
  This is a great bedtime snack, as rolled oats provide sleep-inducing amino acids and B vitamins.

- **Natural cherries**
  For a melatonin boost. Have a few on their own, or add to granola with some plant-based yogurt.

- **Walnuts**
  Another good source of melatonin—make some simple energy balls (see page 132) and keep them in the freezer.

- **Hummus on crackers or toast**
  Chickpea hummus contains tryptophan, which is an amino acid that gets converted into melatonin in the body. Spread on rye toast or crackers.

Calming miso pasta

This is a quick dish with minimum prep—perfect for when you need to prioritize time for rest. Miso is nourishing and comforting and, being made from fermented soybeans, it has benefits for our gut, too. There have been many links made between a healthy gut and maintaining positive emotions, so this is a truly holistic approach to feeling rested. Pasta is one of the ultimate comfort foods, and so a big bowl of this will leave you feeling wonderfully relaxed.

---

1 lb 2 oz butternut squash, peeled, cut into ¾-inch dice

10½ oz pasta (I like whole wheat tagliatelle)

3 garlic cloves, chopped

a glug of olive oil

5 cups spinach

3 tbsp white miso paste

½ a chopped fresh chile

1 tbsp rice vinegar

3 tbsp any nut butter (I like almond)

sea salt and freshly ground black pepper

a squeeze of fresh lime, to serve

a handful of sliced almonds (or any nuts, chopped), to serve

Preheat the oven to 400°F. Line a roasting pan with parchment paper. Roast the butternut squash on the lined baking pan (no need to add any oil) for 25 minutes, until soft.

While the squash is in the oven, cook the pasta in a large pot of salted water, according to the package instructions, then drain.

In a large bowl, mash the cooked butternut squash until smooth.

In a small skillet, lightly fry the garlic in the olive oil for a minute or so, then add the spinach and cook until just wilted. Tip into the bowl with the squash, then add the miso paste, chile, rice vinegar, nut butter, and a splash of water. Mix together until really creamy. Season to taste with salt and pepper, then gently fold in the pasta until well coated.

Serve in bowls with a squeeze of fresh lime and sprinkled sliced almonds.

Wild mushrooms on toast with tamari and thyme

When we feel completely exhausted, tasty things on toast are the ultimate shortcut to a quick and nourishing meal. Even better, you'll probably have most of the ingredients for this in your pantry and fridge already. Mushrooms are full of magnesium, which can help us feel calmer and less anxious. Don't worry if you can't find wild mushrooms—regular mushrooms will work just as well.

a glug of olive oil

2 shallots (or 1 small onion), finely sliced

sea salt and freshly ground black pepper

14 oz mixed mushrooms (shiitake and wild mushrooms are great, but any mushrooms will do), wiped clean and sliced—feel free to leave some of the smaller wild mushrooms whole, as they are so pretty

5 cups spinach

2 garlic cloves, chopped

a few sprigs of fresh thyme, leaves picked

1 tbsp tamari

½ tsp hot paprika or chile powder

a handful of freshly chopped parsley

juice of 1 lemon

2 thick slices of sourdough bread

toasted nuts or seeds, to serve (*optional*)

In a large frying pan, heat the olive oil over medium heat, then add the shallots. Sprinkle with salt and cook for about 5 minutes, until the shallots begin to soften.

Add the mushrooms, making sure they don't crowd the pan. Toss with the shallots to coat in the oil, then cook for a couple of minutes. Add the spinach, garlic, thyme, tamari, and paprika and season with salt and pepper. Leave for 2 to 3 minutes, then give the pan a good shake and stir in most of the parsley and the lemon juice.

While the mushrooms are cooking, toast the bread. Place the toast on plates and pile high with the mushrooms. Sprinkle with some toasted nuts or seeds for some extra crunch if you fancy and sprinkle with the rest of the parsley.

Change it up by stirring in ¾ cup plus 2 tbsp plant-based natural yogurt. Serve with rice as a stroganoff!

Sleepy rice pudding

This is the most comforting rice pudding ever. Chamomile has been used for years as a natural relaxant and sedative, and along with the rich coconut rice this is the perfect food to help you drift off into a restful sleep. The process of making this pudding is also very therapeutic; be mindful as you stir the rice to achieve the perfect creamy consistency. It's a meditation in itself!

½ cup jasmine rice, rinsed well and drained
1 (13.5 oz/400 ml) can coconut milk
1 chamomile tea bag brewed in ¼ cup plus 3 tbsp hot water
sea salt
a handful of raisins
2 tbsp maple syrup
1 tsp ground cinnamon
1 tsp fresh chamomile flowers to garnish (*optional*)

Put the rice in a medium saucepan and pour in just enough water to cover it. Place the pan over medium heat and once it has started to boil, turn the heat down to medium-low and let it cook gently for 10 minutes. Take care not to let the water evaporate completely—keep an eye on the pan and top it up if necessary. Drain the rice and return it to the pan.

Add the coconut milk, chamomile tea, and a pinch of salt and cook on medium-low heat for 25 minutes, stirring every few minutes to make sure the rice doesn't stick.

Add the raisins and maple syrup and turn the heat to low. Cook for another 15 minutes, stirring frequently, until creamy. Serve with a sprinkle of cinnamon on top and garnish with the chamomile flowers, if using.

 Swap the chamomile tea for some tart cherry juice (no added sugar) and a few fresh or frozen cherries.

REST WELL,
SLEEP WELL

When we are stressed or have a million things going around our minds, it can be hard to drop off to sleep. Or maybe you can get to sleep without much of a problem but find yourself wide awake a couple of hours later staring at the ceiling. . . . Of course, if there's something specific worrying you and keeping you awake, then the best solution is to try and resolve that issue once and for all. But in the meantime, or if that's just not possible right now, try these simple steps for achieving a deeply restful night's sleep so you wake up feeling rejuvenated.

Make a sleep oil

Mix ¼ cup plus 3 tbsp sweet almond oil (which you can buy at most health food stores) with 3 or 4 drops each of lavender essential oil, which is good for relaxation; ylang-ylang essential oil, known for its antianxiety properties; and cedarwood essential oil, believed to be a natural muscle relaxant and mild sedative. Or use 10 drops of your favorite relaxing essential oil. Shake together, then apply to your skin after a warm bath before bed to help you drift off into a dreamy sleep.

Write your worries down

Whether you're already into journaling or if you've just had a stressful day and need to clear your head, write down whatever thoughts you have racing around, then set them aside for the night.

Create a calming sleep environment

- *Let your bedroom breathe.* Open the windows and get some fresh air in every day .

- *Burn relaxing essential oils* to make your room smell divine.

- *Reduce the clutter.* Give your room a good cleanout and get rid of those odd socks you have hiding under the bed!

- *Invest in some new bedding.* It doesn't need to cost a fortune—you can get some on sale—but it really makes a difference.

- *Keep colors and artwork peaceful.* Set the mood for relaxation.

- *Keep it dark.* Even a little artificial light can upset your natural sleep cycle. Think about investing in blackout blinds or wear an eye mask.

- *No late-night scrolling!* We all know the blue light emitted from electronics can affect sleep, but social media can sometimes spark negative thought processes, too. You want to go to bed feeling calm and content.

calm

That feeling of being tranquil, with the absence of any strong emotions or stressful thought patterns, is such a nice idea, isn't it? But daily life, chores, family commitments, and worries can often mean that calm isn't something we feel or practice often enough. Maybe we have even forgotten what it actually feels like to be calm?

As a first step, try to include just five minutes of calm in your busy day by closing your eyes and focusing on your breathing. See opposite for my calming breath-work exercise. It's such a simple practice but has huge and long-lasting effects. It can be done anywhere and at any time when you are feeling anxious or frantic. Try it before you leave the house in the morning to help set a calm intention for the day, or when you get back at night to reset before the evening.

In this section, I have chosen recipes based on ingredients that can relieve stress and anxiety, to help you realize that longed-for sense of calm. When you are feeling overwhelmed, I know that cooking can sometimes feel like yet another thing that you need to do, but try to enjoy the process. Preparing a meal for yourself—and for others—is incredibly nourishing and a wonderful act of self-care. Cooking can be such a calming and enjoyable activity—a kind of meditation therapy in itself. See page 44 for more on mindful cooking.

Being kind to yourself and allowing yourself a few moments of tranquility and peace during the day is something you deserve and need in order to calm your mind and help balance your emotions, so make sure to factor it in.

5-MINUTE CALMING
BREATH WORK

1. Sit or lie in a comfortable position and breathe in deeply and slowly through your nose.

2. Purse your lips as you breathe out through your mouth, making sure to keep your jaw relaxed.

3. Repeat, focusing on your breath for five minutes—or longer if you have time and can manage it! Don't worry if your mind wanders, just draw your attention back to the breath.

OVERNIGHT OATS

Keep a jar of rolled oats on the shelf and with just five minutes of prep, you'll have a nourishing breakfast waiting for you the next day. Rolled oats are rich in fiber, magnesium, and B vitamins, as well as being a source of slow-release energy, so they are a one-hit wonder in terms of calming an anxious mind. Just use rolled oats and plant-based milk with a little fresh fruit and honey, or add a little cinnamon and vanilla for an extra flavor boost. Chia seeds will provide extra protein and healthy fats. Other tasty additions include a generous spoonful of nut butter, a sprinkling of granola (see page 19), or mix in some magical superfood powders, such as spirulina, cacao, or maca powder.

Basic overnight oats recipe

½ cup rolled oats
½ cup plant-based milk, such as almond
    or coconut
1 tbsp honey (or maple syrup)
a handful of fresh fruit (e.g., berries, chopped
    banana, grated apple, or chopped peaches)

OPTIONAL EXTRAS
a pinch of ground cinnamon
½ tsp vanilla extract
1 tbsp chia seeds
1 tbsp nut butter
1 tbsp shredded coconut
1 to 2 tbsp granola (see my recipe on page 19)

Combine the oats and plant-based milk
in a small jar or bowl and stir in the
honey or maple syrup. If you are using
cinnamon, vanilla, chia seeds, or nut
butter, stir these in now, too. Cover and
leave in the fridge overnight.

The next morning, top with fresh fruit,
shredded coconut, and granola, if
using. If you want to make your oats a
little thinner, stir in a splash more milk
before you add the toppings.

• MACA MOOD BOOSTER

Maca is amazing for balancing
hormones, helping with PMS symptoms,
and menopause. It is also a great stress
reliever. Bananas boost serotonin, our
happy hormone.

1 tbsp maca powder, stirred into the oat mix
the next day, served with 1 chopped banana.

• GREEN ENERGY BOOST

Spirulina is great for energy and is full of
nutrients and vitamins. It also contains
tryptophan, an amino acid that supports
serotonin production.

2 tsp spirulina powder, stirred into the oat mix
the next day, served with chopped green fruits
(such as kiwi, grapes, or apple).

• CHILL-OUT CHERRY

Cherries are one of only a few natural
food sources of melatonin. Raw cacao
can help reduce anxiety—it is rich in
antioxidants, vitamins, and minerals.

1 tsp cacao powder, stirred into the oat mix
the next day, served with a small handful of
fresh or frozen cherries (defrosted if frozen),
pitted and chopped.

Roasted roots happy salad

This colorful warm salad is full of ingredients to help us feel calmer. Walnuts are a great source of omega-3 and selenium—if we are lacking in the mineral selenium, we can feel depressed or anxious, so it's a great idea to add a few walnuts (or Brazil nuts) to your meals when you can. I believe you eat and feast with your eyes first, and this dish is so beautiful to look at, too, and will leave you feeling wonderfully relaxed.

2 carrots, quartered
  lengthwise
2 parsnips, peeled and
  quartered lengthwise
2 small red onions,
  quartered
2 small raw beets, peeled
  and cut into chunks
1 small red bell pepper,
  sliced into large chunks
a glug of olive oil
1 tbsp honey
sea salt and freshly ground
  black pepper
4 garlic cloves (not peeled)
1¾ cups walnuts
3⅓ cups spinach
a bunch of parsley,
  chopped
1 tbsp pomegranate seeds
edible flowers, such as
  nasturtiums, primroses,
  and chive flowers, to
  garnish (*optional*)

For the dressing
1 garlic clove, chopped
1 tbsp mustard
5 tbsp raw apple cider
  vinegar
2 tbsp lemon juice
1 to 2 tbsp honey, to taste
7 tbsp extra-virgin olive oil
sea salt and freshly ground
  black pepper, to taste

Preheat the oven to 425°F. Line a roasting pan with
parchment paper.

Put the carrots, parsnips, red onions, beets, and
bell pepper in a bowl and toss in some olive oil, the
honey, and some salt and pepper to taste. Spread the
vegetables out in the lined pan with the garlic and
cook for 35 to 40 minutes, until tender. When cool
enough to handle, peel the garlic and set aside.

Meanwhile, in a dry frying pan set over medium
heat, gently cook the walnuts, tossing them
regularly, until they turn a darker brown color.
It should only take a few minutes—do not leave them
or they will burn! Tip them onto a plate to cool a
little.

To make the dressing, whisk all the ingredients
together in a small bowl.

Put the spinach, parsley, and walnuts in a large
serving bowl and add the cooked veggies along
with the garlic and all the juices from the roasting
pan. Toss well to coat. Finish with a sprinkle of
pomegranate seeds and drizzle the dressing over
the top.

Garnish with the edible flowers, if using.

 Any leftover veg is delicious in a wrap or sandwich.

Mindful ramen

Even the process of making ramen relaxes me. Take a moment to pause and enjoy this bowl of food before you eat it. Stopping, being mindful and taking a breath just to appreciate what is around us can be instantly grounding and calming for the body and mind. Add as many raw, bright veggies as you like—the different colors always cheer me up! Shiitake mushrooms are full of B vitamins to boost your mood and reduce stress.

1 tbsp miso paste
a handful of dried seaweed (*optional*)
a handful of dried shiitake mushrooms
a slice of fresh ginger
1 tbsp tamari
2½ oz noodles (such as buckwheat or soba)
1 tsp coconut or olive oil
3½ oz firm tofu (I use chickpea tofu, but any firm tofu will do), sliced thickly
2 handfuls of raw chopped veggies (such as bok choy, bean sprouts, sliced carrots, spinach, and radish)

To serve
1 chopped fresh chile (if you like it hot)

Put the miso paste, seaweed (if using), mushrooms, and 1 quart water in a saucepan on high heat and bring to a boil. Add the ginger and tamari, reduce the heat, and simmer for 10 minutes.

In a separate saucepan, cook the noodles in boiling water for 6 to 7 minutes, or according to the instructions on the package. Drain and set aside.

Meanwhile, heat the oil in a frying pan and lightly fry the tofu for 2 minutes on each side, then set aside.

Strain the broth into a bowl, using a sieve. Put the cooked noodles and the raw veggies into the bottom of two soup bowls and pour the broth over the top. Slice some of the mushrooms and seaweed from the strained broth and add to the ramen. Top with the tofu and scatter with the chopped chile, if using.

 Freeze the strained broth in batches for future ramen-making or to use as a tasty stock for soups and stews.

SERVES 4 | Prep time: 15 minutes | Cooking time: 15 minutes, plus 4 hours to chill

Indulgent chocolate pudding

Cherries are a natural source of melatonin to help your sleep and keep you feeling calm. And, of course, we all know what a mood booster cacao can be! This decadent pudding is packed with nutrients, including magnesium, which is essential for helping you feel rested.

⅔ cup fresh or frozen
  cherries, defrosted
  if frozen, pitted, and
  chopped
2 tbsp maple syrup
3½ oz dark chocolate
1 cup coconut cream
2 tbsp coconut oil
1 tsp vanilla extract
2 tbsp cacao powder

To serve (*optional*)
grated chocolate
whole cherries
edible flowers

Add the cherries to a saucepan set over low heat with ¼ cup and 3 tbsp water and 1 tbsp maple syrup. Cook on low for a few minutes, until the cherries are soft. Remove from the heat, drain, and leave to cool.

Place a small heatproof bowl over a pot of gently simmering water. Break the chocolate into the bowl and leave until melted, stirring occasionally. Set aside.

Put the coconut cream, coconut oil, remaining maple syrup, and vanilla in a small saucepan and heat, but do not bring to a boil, stirring constantly.

Pour the melted chocolate into the coconut mixture along with the cacao powder and mix well, then stir in the cherries. Spoon into small jars, glasses, or bowls and chill in the fridge for about 4 hours.

When you're ready to serve, decorate with grated chocolate and a whole cherry or an edible flower.

 You can swap the cherries for any berries.

MINDFUL COOKING

Being more mindful as we go about our everyday activities can help us feel happier. If we reframe our daily chores as mindfulness meditations, suddenly even vacuuming the stairs can become a calming and restorative exercise! Maybe. . . . For most people, cooking dinner can be a stressful, hurried, last-minute grab-and-panic to feed the kids or put something on the table before it gets too late. Obviously, some nights will always be like this, but try inviting a bit more awareness into the process of preparing a meal, even if at first it's only on the weekend, when you have more time.

Do you feel frustrated when you're making a new dish?

Feeling stressed about getting the ingredients together or how it's going to turn out will set the tone before you even start! Stay present and mindful throughout the process and try to enjoy every stage of it—from sourcing the ingredients to prepping the veggies. You may not be a MasterChef and the recipe might not even turn out as planned, but that's completely OK and part of the fun. The whole process is there to be enjoyed—and you might even invent something new! Try to approach cooking as a creative endeavor rather than something that simply has to "get done." When you adopt a positive mindset, cooking can be something you find genuine pleasure in.

Be grateful for the wonderful food we have access to

As you shop and prepare the ingredients, think about where they have come from—who helped grow them? What were the processes involved in their arriving in your kitchen? Did you buy them from your local fruit and veg stall or farmers' market, or were they flown in from the other side of the world? Think about every step they took to get to you. Being more mindful as we shop might even lead us to think about the impact our choices have on our local community and the wider world.

Consider each of your senses as you cook

Really focus in on them. What do the veggies feel like as you chop them? Listen to the sound of the frying onions. How does it smell when you throw all those lovely spices into the pan? How do the contrasting colors look when you serve up the finished dish? When we tune in like this it can really help us appreciate every step of the cooking process.

cozy

Cozy is my favorite word of all time, and it makes me feel happy just thinking of it. For me, being cozy feels like a hug and a warm blanket. Cozy feels safe and it is exactly where I want to be at the end of a long day.

Obviously, a big, thick blanket and hot mug of tea will help, but we need to experience that cozy and content feeling in our mind, too. We need to switch off from the day and slow down our whirring brain, which might still be running through all the things on our to-do list. Simply by focusing on something that makes us feel happy and content—like a favorite photo— or by lighting a few candles and getting into some cozy socks, we can create a welcoming environment that can encourage us into that warm, contented frame of mind.

On the following pages are my ultimate recipes to help get you into that cozy place, using ingredients that will calm a racing mind and boost your mood by encouraging the production of your feel-good hormone serotonin.

But don't just save cozy for home—here are my top tips for getting cozy wherever you are:

- **Loose clothing.** Think big sweaters and cozy scarves in winter, and floaty dresses and soft fabrics in summer. There's nothing cozy about feeling restricted in tight clothes.

- **A favorite chair.** Find a perfect comfy spot either at home or in your local café and go there whenever you need a bit of peace and a few moments to enjoy a quiet cup of tea.

- **Listen up.** When you're traveling in rush hour or doing the grocery shopping, it might seem impossible to feel cozy and relaxed. Block out everyone around you by putting on your headphones and listening to some feel-good music or to your favorite comedian for a bit of instant laughter therapy.

- **Warm and happy vibes.** We all have things going on in our lives, but just for a few moments, put your worries aside and focus on the good stuff.

HOT DRINKS

I'm not sure there are many things more comforting or cozy than a hot drink. In the morning, I like to drink a cup of hot water with a slice of lemon and ginger to help wake up my digestive system, and during the day I often just pop a couple of sprigs of herbs (like rosemary or thyme) in a mug, pour in boiling water and let it infuse for a few minutes. Here are some of my favorite hugs-in-mugs drinks to enjoy at any time.

• Chamomile and honey latte

For years chamomile tea has been used as a natural remedy to reduce anxiety and treat insomnia, so this is the perfect bedtime drink.

1 chamomile tea bag
½ cup plus 2 tbsp plant-based milk
½ tbsp honey
ground cinnamon, to serve

In a mug, brew the tea bag in ¼ cup plus 3 tbsp boiling water for 5 to 10 minutes. Meanwhile, heat the milk in a small saucepan over medium heat. Whisk constantly until warm and frothy. Discard the tea bag, add the honey, and stir. Pour in the frothed milk and top with ground cinnamon.

• Soothing golden milk

This soothing creamy drink is great if you're feeling under the weather as the spices will help fight off colds and boost your immune system.

1 cup plant-based milk
2 tsp honey or maple syrup
2 tsp almond butter
½ tsp vanilla extract
½ tsp ground cinnamon
¼ tsp ground turmeric
¼ tsp ground ginger
¼ tsp ground cardamom
a pinch of freshly ground black pepper

Warm all the ingredients in a small saucepan over medium heat, whisking constantly so the almond butter doesn't stick to the bottom and the spices mix in.

• Mood-boosting hot chocolate

The mood-boosting effects of cacao really are true! Chocolate stimulates the brain, in turn releasing feel-good hormones. Avoid this close to bedtime though. Top with crushed hazelnuts, coconut, or dark chocolate.

1 tsp coconut oil
1 cup plant-based milk
1 tbsp cacao powder
½ tsp ground turmeric
½ tsp vanilla extract
1 tbsp maple syrup
½ tsp ground cinnamon
a pinch of freshly ground black pepper

In a small saucepan, whisk the coconut oil with the milk over medium heat until just boiling. Add all ingredients to a blender and blitz until smooth. Alternatively, whisk together in the saucepan; it won't be as frothy. Add a little more maple syrup, if desired.

49

Fiery bean stew

If you're feeling a bit under the weather, the ginger and cayenne in this dish can help nip coughs or colds in the bud before they take hold. The spinach adds extra iron, but swap it for kale or chard if you fancy a change. A big bowl of this is really all you need to leave you feeling all warm and cozy, restoring you from the inside out!

a glug of olive oil
1 small onion, sliced
1 leek, sliced
2 garlic cloves, chopped
1 inch fresh ginger, peeled
  and chopped
a pinch of cayenne
3 carrots, sliced
1 (14.5-oz) can diced tomatoes
1 tsp honey
1¼ cups veggie stock (see
  page 18 for homemade)
1 tbsp tamari
5 cups spinach
2 (15-oz) cans lima beans,
  drained and rinsed
a handful of freshly
  chopped parsley
a handful of roughly
  chopped basil
sea salt and freshly ground
  black pepper
bread, to serve
cooked quinoa, to serve
  (optional)

Heat a glug of olive oil in a large saucepan over medium heat. Add the onion and leek and cook for 2 to 3 minutes, then add the garlic, ginger, cayenne, and carrots. Cook for 2 minutes before adding the tomatoes, honey, stock, and tamari. Bring to a simmer and bubble for 5 minutes.

Stir in the spinach and beans, then simmer for 10 minutes until hot. Stir in the fresh herbs and season with salt and pepper. Serve in bowls with cooked quinoa and a hunk of yummy bread.

 Swap the lima beans for any type of beans you like, such as kidney beans or cannellini beans, or replace with chickpeas or red lentils.

SERVES 4 | Prep time: 10 minutes | Cooking time: 1 hour

Comfort pie

This pie does exactly what it says! It is an old favorite of mine, and something I started making when the kids were small, but I've added a few more spices here to please my taste buds. You know when you've been on a long walk and your cheeks are stinging from the wind and you get home and all you want is something to warm your cockles and make you feel cozy? Well, this is that dish. Full of mood-boosting ingredients, it's the ultimate wholesome dinner for anyone who needs some comfort.

For the mashed potato topping

12 oz potatoes, chopped
14 oz sweet potatoes, chopped
sea salt and freshly ground black pepper
3 tbsp plant-based milk
3 tbsp olive oil

For the filling

3 tbsp olive oil
1 medium onion, chopped
2 garlic cloves, chopped
1 leek, chopped
2 celery stalks, chopped
1 carrot, chopped into smallish chunks
1 tsp smoked paprika
1 tsp ground cinnamon
1 (15-oz) can kidney beans
1 (15-oz) can cannellini beans
1 (15-oz) can chickpeas
¾ cup dried red lentils
1 (14.5-oz) can diced tomatoes
1¼ cups veggie stock (see page 18 for homemade)
2 bay leaves
sea salt and freshly ground black pepper
1 tbsp tamari
2 tsp dried thyme
a handful of parsley leaves
mixed salad, tossed in olive oil and a pinch of sea salt, to serve

First make the mash. Bring a large saucepan of water to a boil. Add all the potatoes and a pinch of sea salt and cook for 20 minutes, until soft.

While the potatoes are cooking, heat 3 tbsp olive oil in another large saucepan set over medium heat. Cook the onion and garlic for 2 minutes, until starting to soften. Add the leek, celery, and carrot and continue cooking on low heat for about 5 minutes, until they soften.

Add the paprika, cinnamon, kidney and cannellini beans, chickpeas, lentils, and tomatoes. Give the mix a really good stir, then add the stock and bay leaves. Season with salt and pepper and simmer on low for 15 minutes, until the lentils are soft. (Add a little extra water if it's starting to look too thick—it should have the consistency of a shepherd's pie filling.)

Preheat the oven to 400°F.

Drain the spuds and return them to the saucepan (a large bowl is OK, too). Add the plant-based milk and 3 tbsp olive oil, and mash with a potato masher until smooth. Season with salt and pepper.

Stir the tamari, thyme, and parsley into the beans mixture and spoon it into a large pie dish (remove the bay leaves if you can find them!). Spread it out evenly and top with the mashed potatoes. Run a fork through the topping and bake for 35 to 40 minutes, until the edges of the topping are crispy and the pie is heated through.

Serve with the mixed salad.

 You can make the mashed topping with any root veg, such as carrots or parsnips, or try it with cauliflower.

Spiced ginger cake

Not too naughty and very nice, this is a real taste of luxury when served with some plant-based custard or ice cream. It's also great for getting cozy with a cup of tea as an afternoon treat. The homemade applesauce is a brilliant way to use up any leftover apples in your fruit bowl.

For the applesauce

8 oz cooking apples,
  peeled, cored, and
  chopped
zest and juice of 1 lemon
1 tsp brown sugar
1 cinnamon stick
sea salt

For the cake

2⅔ cups whole wheat flour
packed ½ cup plus 1 tbsp
  brown sugar
2 tsp baking powder
2 tsp ground ginger
1 tsp ground cinnamon
¼ tsp ground cloves
2 tbsp chopped crystallized
  ginger
generous ¾ cup pitted and
  chopped dates
¾ cup applesauce
  (homemade, above, or
  store-bought)
3 tbsp plant-based milk
juice of 1 lemon
1 tsp vanilla extract

To serve

1 tbsp peanut butter
1 tbsp maple syrup

To make the applesauce, put the chopped apples in a large saucepan. Add 2 tablespoons water, the lemon zest and juice, sugar, cinnamon, and a pinch of salt. Stir well. Cook for 15 minutes on medium heat, stirring occasionally, until the apples are mushy, then remove from the heat, discarding the cinnamon stick.

Preheat the oven to 375°F. Line an 8½ by 4½-inch loaf pan with parchment paper.

In a large bowl, mix together all the dry ingredients, including the crystallized ginger and dates. Add the applesauce, plant-based milk, lemon juice, and vanilla extract and give it a good stir.

Using a rubber spatula, pour into the prepared pan and smooth the top. Bake for about 50 minutes, until a toothpick inserted into the middle comes out perfectly clean.

In a small pan, warm the peanut butter and maple syrup on low heat, stirring to combine well. Drizzle over the hot cake before slicing and serving.

INSTANT COZINESS

Get comfy

Take off those tight jeans or high-waisted leggings that pull your tummy in (why do I wear these!) and throw on the coziest, baggiest, comfiest clothes you own. I normally go for my slightly battered—but deliciously soft—cotton yoga pants and a chunky knitted sweater I've had for years. Why do you get so much comfort from that old sweater you've had for years? Maybe because it brings back pleasurable feelings of home, of being loved, and happy nostalgic memories, which are definitely good for the soul.

Feel comfy in your own skin

This is everything. To feel cozy from within, we really need to accept our true selves. Taking charge of your thoughts can be so tough. We are our own biggest critics, but instead of picking out flaws and putting yourself down, embrace yourself for who you are and love your unique, beautiful being. Honor your body, too—it really is so important to celebrate every part of you and feel positive about how you look. These simple steps can help you maintain a healthy and positive mind, leading to a happy spirit.

Let yourself have a break

It's important to allow yourself to be cozy. Don't be hard on yourself for having a moment of not doing anything. There is so much pressure to be busy that sometimes we forget to stop, or don't allow ourselves to. Get cozy and enjoy it without feeling guilty. Light some candles and have a hot bath in the middle of the day. Why not? Watch your favorite film or read that book that's been sitting on your bedside table for ages. Give yourself permission to do whatever it is you need to do to wind down and relax.

BE STILL

1. Find your favorite chair or corner of the sofa and snuggle up—maybe with a blanket. Or you may prefer to sit outside in the garden in the fresh air. For me, it has to be my bedroom; it's definitely the quietest room in the house (when the kids don't invade), and it also has the most natural sunlight.

2. Once you've found your cozy place, just sit or lie down, and be still. That is it. Nothing else needs to happen.

3. Focus on your breathing and only that (maybe try the breathing exercise on page 35). When the thoughts and lists and stress start creeping back in, just acknowledge them and then let them go, and go back to being still.

Rebalance

From time to time it can feel as though life has shifted off-balance. Maybe we've taken on too much at work, or our calendar is filled with social occasions we can't even remember committing to. Sometimes we can want to do all these things, but after a while we start to feel unstable and wobbly. If this feels like you, then it's important to find a little time to put yourself first and think about what you can do to bring things back into balance.

When life feels overwhelming, start with some small positive changes, so you can start to take control of the situation. First, get a sense of what the areas are in your life that you feel need more balance. Writing a list is a great, practical way to approach this. Seeing things written down in black and white is a surprisingly effective way to create order amid the seeming chaos.

Try asking yourself these questions:

- *What am I doing too much of?*
- *What would I like to do more of?*
- *What areas of my self-care have I let slide?*
- *Am I eating well, or is there too much sugar, caffeine, or takeout in my diet?*
- *Do I need to make more time for fun?*

Once you have a better idea of what is making things feel out of kilter, you can then go about redressing the balance. Maybe you need to say no to something you would usually agree to. Perhaps you need to get outside more and simply enjoy some fresh air and being in nature. Have you lost touch with friends because you all seem so busy all the time? Maybe you just need to introduce a bit more fun and joy into your day-to-day.

connected

When we feel alone or disconnected from a loved one or the family unit, it can really affect our daily life and leave us experiencing a sense of isolation. The connections we make with family, friends, neighbors, colleagues, and even our pets all help bring us together in a circle of closeness that makes us feel supported and loved. Maintaining those relationships that really mean something to us is essential to our overall well-being, and we should make sure to take time to nurture them.

Connections can so easily fall away, especially in this crazy world we live in where we spend so much time on our phones and looking through social media. So it's really important to keep the relationships real by talking and communicating. Even simply sitting around the dinner table as a family (no phones allowed) is a great way of sharing feelings and daily experiences; it gives us a chance to find out what's going on with each other.

Adulthood and all the responsibilities it brings can mean socializing with our friends just doesn't happen as often as we would like. But it's vital to keep those friendships alive and the connections strong. Maybe it means catching up on the phone every now and again or planning a yearly get-together instead of those once-weekly clubbing sessions, but it doesn't matter, because with true friends you don't have to see them all the time to know they are there.

The recipes in this section are all about encouraging connection. They are my favorite sharing plates for plonking in the middle of the table and serving out among yourselves. As you all dig in and eat together, these dishes will help create a shared feeling of connection around your table.

Jackfruit taco party

Sharing food around a table is one of life's great pleasures, and this is the meal I always want to make if I have friends or family over. It's so much fun, and everyone gets to make their own personal taco! The trick with these is to have fun and don't worry if you get a little messy—and to have a stack of paper towels on hand! Jackfruit is a great meat substitute; it absorbs flavors really well and has a texture similar to pulled pork once cooked. (You could buy a good-quality BBQ sauce if you prefer, but this one is really delicious.)

For the filling

2 (14-oz) cans jackfruit in
    brine, drained
2 tsp garlic powder
2 tsp smoked paprika
4 tsp liquid smoke (see
    page 11)
sea salt and freshly ground
    black pepper
a glug of olive oil
2 small red onions, sliced
2 small bell peppers,
    seeded and sliced
8 taco shells (2 each)

For the BBQ sauce

½ (14.5-oz) can diced
    tomatoes
2 tbsp tomato paste
1 tbsp molasses (or maple
    syrup)
packed ¼ cup brown sugar
1 tbsp raw apple cider
    vinegar
2 tsp chile powder
1 tsp onion powder
1 tsp garlic powder
1 tsp smoked paprika
½ tsp mustard
a pinch of sea salt

To serve

¼ small red cabbage, thinly
    sliced
3⅓ cups spinach
1 tomato, chopped
cilantro leaves
lime wedges

Put the drained jackfruit in an airtight container.
Add the garlic powder, paprika, liquid smoke, and
some salt and pepper, and mix until well coated.
Use the back of a fork to shred the jackfruit. (There
will be small, soft seeds that you can eat, too.)
Leave to marinate in the fridge for at least 2 hours,
but preferably overnight.

Once ready to cook, preheat the oven to 425°F. Line
a baking sheet with parchment paper.

Heat the oil in a large frying pan over low heat.
Cook the onions and peppers for about 10 minutes,
until they are soft and caramelizing a little. Add the
jackfruit and cook for another 10 minutes, stirring
every so often.

Spread the mixture onto the lined baking sheet and
roast for 15 minutes.

While the jackfruit is cooking, make your BBQ sauce.
Place all the ingredients in a small saucepan and cook
over medium heat for 5 minutes.

To assemble the tacos, layer each shell with cabbage,
spinach, and chopped tomato. Load the jackfruit
mixture on top. Generously drizzle with the BBQ sauce
and finish with the cilantro and a squeeze of lime.

*Add a drained and rinsed 15-oz can of kidney beans
and a 14.5 oz can of diced tomatoes to the jackfruit
mixture and heat through for a spicy jackfruit chili to
serve with rice.*

Smoky stuffed eggplants

This is a really great sharing dish—especially because you can prepare it way in advance and keep it in the fridge all day. Then it just needs a five-minute broil to cook through at the end. It is a wonderfully balanced dish in terms of its flavors, too, with warming spices, freshness from the lemon zest, and plant-based yogurt to cool things down.

2 eggplants, halved lengthwise and flesh scored
3 garlic cloves, crushed
olive oil
sea salt and freshly ground black pepper
½ cup wild rice
1 medium onion, finely sliced
1 red chile, seeded and finely chopped
2 tsp smoked paprika
½ cup sun-dried tomatoes, rehydrated (or from a jar in olive oil), chopped
1 tsp harissa
zest and juice of 1 lemon
a bunch of parsley, chopped
1¼ cups walnuts, chopped
breadcrumbs from 2 slices of bread (blitz them in a blender)

To serve
¼ cup plus 3 tbsp plant-based plain yogurt
a bunch of fresh mint, chopped
1 fresh chile, chopped
a pinch of sea salt
mixed green salad leaves

Preheat the oven to 425°F. Spread the scored surface of the eggplants with half of the garlic and drizzle with a little olive oil. Season really well with salt and pepper. Put them on a baking sheet and cook in the oven for 30 minutes, then set aside.

While the eggplants are in the oven, put the rice in a saucepan with 1 quart cold water and a pinch of salt. Bring to a boil, then decrease the heat. With the lid on, cook for 20 minutes. Drain and set aside.

Heat a glug of olive oil in a saucepan and cook the onion, chile, and the rest of the garlic for 5 minutes, until soft. Stir in the paprika and cook for another minute. Add the sun-dried tomatoes, harissa, lemon zest and juice, parsley, walnuts, and cooked rice and give it a really good mix.

Scoop the flesh from the eggplants, being careful not to break the skin. Add the eggplant flesh to the rice and give it another good mix. Now you need to stuff the eggplant skins with the rice mixture.

Preheat the broiler. Top the eggplants with the breadcrumbs and another drizzle of olive oil and broil for 5 minutes.

To serve, drizzle the plant-based yogurt over the top and sprinkle with the chopped mint and chile and some salt. Serve with the green salad.

Eggplants are wonderful veggies and are available all year round, though they are at their best in the summer. If you can't find good ones, use bell peppers instead. You could also swap the sun-dried tomatoes for chopped pitted olives.

Life's a peach (and almond tart)

Life is all about balance and that includes treating ourselves from time to time! Roasting the peaches for this tasty tart takes a little while, so this is one for a relaxed Sunday afternoon gathering. It really melts in the mouth— and you can add an extra layer of decadence with a generous amount of plant-based ice cream or custard.

For the pastry

1⅔ cups all-purpose flour
    (or 1¾ cups whole wheat
    flour), sifted, plus more for
    dusting
a pinch of sea salt
1 tsp ground cinnamon
2 tbsp confectioners' sugar
¼ cup olive oil
a little coconut or olive oil,
    for greasing

For the filling

2 cups ground almonds
packed ⅓ cup brown sugar
1 tsp ground cinnamon
3 tbsp almond milk
1 tsp almond extract
3 or 4 ripe peaches, sliced
    evenly
2 tbsp peach or apricot jam,
    dissolved in ¼ cup water
    to make a glaze
a handful of chopped
    toasted almonds
    (*optional*)

Line an 8-inch round cake pan with parchment paper and grease with a little coconut or olive oil. In a bowl, whisk together the flour, salt, cinnamon, and confectioners' sugar. Add the olive oil and mix with your hands to form crumbs. Add 3 tablespoons water and bring together into a dough. (Add a little more water if needed.) Flour your work surface, then roll out the dough into a circle about ¼ inch thick. Chill on a lined baking sheet in the fridge for about 1 hour.

Preheat the oven to 400°F. In a bowl, combine the ground almonds, sugar, cinnamon, almond milk, and almond extract.

Remove the pastry from the fridge and arrange it on the bottom of the cake pan. Spread the filling across the dough, leaving a ¾-inch border around the outside. Arrange the peach slices on top, making sure there are no gaps between the slices. Pinch the pastry around the fruit. (You can trim the edges, but I like a rustic look.)

Using a pastry brush or the back of a small spoon, apply half the apricot glaze to the pastry and fruit. Cover with foil and bake for 45 minutes, then remove the foil and cook for another 15 minutes to allow the pastry to brown. Once out of the oven, top with the remaining glaze and chopped almonds, if desired.

| Find your tribe

TOGETHERNESS

Togetherness could mean sitting round a huge dinner table with all your friends or extended family, feasting on food and laughing and joking until the sun goes down. Or it could mean being with just one other person, holding hands and comforting each other through a time of need. Maybe it even means reaching out and doing something new, and making some new friends along the way.

It's not always easy to put ourselves out there and be around other people, especially if we are feeling unbalanced or caught up in our own head, but it's often just the tonic we need. Being around other people reminds us we're not alone in whatever we are going through, and other people can help bring a fresh perspective on a situation, too.

Meeting new people is always interesting—who knows what they might bring to your life?—but I know that it can sometimes feel a bit nerve-wracking and scary. Getting involved in a creative group is a great way to feel part of a community. Creative activities are also brilliantly therapeutic, enabling you to switch off and think about something else for a while. Perhaps join an art class or writing group—and don't worry about not being any good at it! That's not the point at all. It's about trying new things and feeling surrounded by like-minded people.

Togetherness is also about maintaining a healthy connection between your mind, body, and soul by nurturing your whole self. Making sure you include your physical, mental, emotional, and spiritual needs in your self-care routine can help you feel more "together." Spend time doing a little soul-searching to appreciate what makes you happy. Then surround yourself with people who make you feel like YOU and appreciate all of you—those friends who lift you up and support your dreams, no matter how crazy they may sound. Hold tight to the people who are open-minded and love your quirky ways. When you feel confident and happy after being with them, that's when you'll know you've found your tribe.

nature

Whether you live in the middle of the countryside or in a busy city center, feeling connected to the natural world is essential for our overall well-being. We need to get outside regularly to breathe in the fresh air and feel the breeze on our face.

We all spend so much time indoors these days, at work or looking at screens, that being in nature can definitely get forgotten or slip down the list of what seems important. But, trust me, if you make the effort to get outside, it really will give you such a lift and help you feel more balanced.

Outside walks and mini-hikes will boost natural endorphins, which are the feel-good hormones that improve mood and relieve stress. Simply by surrounding yourself in nature, being out and about in the quiet solitude of the great outdoors, can be incredibly restorative and calming. And if you live in the city, then nature still exists there, even if it's on a smaller scale—most urban areas have much more greenspace than you think, just waiting to be explored. (Also see page 81 for how to get more nature into your life.)

The recipes in this part of the book reflect our need to connect more closely with nature. I've chosen dishes that celebrate Earth's bounty—colorful ingredients combined into wholesome meals to help you get back in touch with what nature can provide.

Creamy sweet potato soup

Sweet potatoes are packed with natural, easy-to-digest carbohydrates and muscle-relaxing potassium. They also contain calcium, which can help us produce sleep-inducing melatonin. The spices and rich color of this soup make it a favorite with everyone I make it for—pure joy in a comforting bowl. Freeze it in portions and reheat gently on the stovetop.

2 lb 4 oz sweet potato, cut into 1¼-inch chunks
1 small onion, cut into wedges
2 garlic cloves
a glug of olive oil
2 tbsp maple syrup
sea salt and freshly ground black pepper
1 tbsp coconut oil
1 tsp cumin seeds
1 tsp coriander seeds
1 tsp red pepper flakes
1 tsp ground turmeric
1 tsp smoked paprika
1 cup veggie stock (see page 18 for homemade)
1 (13.5-oz) can coconut milk

To serve
1 tsp black sesame seeds
sunflower seeds
chopped walnuts
freshly chopped cilantro

Preheat the oven to 400°F. Line a roasting pan with parchment paper. Place the sweet potato, onion, and garlic in the lined pan. Drizzle with olive oil and the maple syrup. Toss to coat and season with salt and pepper. Roast for 25 to 30 minutes, or until golden and tender.

Melt the coconut oil in a large saucepan and lightly toast the seeds and spices for 1 minute. Add the roasted veg and give it all a good stir.

Pour in the veggie stock and coconut milk and season well with salt and pepper. Warm through thoroughly.

In a blender or using a handheld blender, blitz the soup, leaving a little texture. Serve garnished with black sesame seeds, sunflower seeds, chopped walnuts, chopped cilantro, and extra chile flakes if you like it hot.

 When they're in season, use squash or pumpkin instead of sweet potato.

Down-to-earth one-pot stew

A hearty and wonderfully earthy one-pot meal, using lots of fresh herbs, rich lima beans, and mushrooms. It's delicious on its own with a hunk of bread, or serve it at a dinner party with creamy mashed potatoes or some simply cooked rice. Lima beans are a great source of fiber to keep your digestive system healthy. Emotions triggered by stress can have a direct effect on our stomach—and vice versa—so up the fiber in your diet to keep your gut happy. Like any stew, this gets better after a couple of days as the flavors mingle together, so you can make it in advance. It also freezes well.

olive oil
1 lb 2 oz button mushrooms, sliced
1 small onion, thinly sliced
3 garlic cloves, chopped
a small bunch of fresh thyme, leaves picked
2 sprigs of fresh rosemary, leaves picked and chopped
2 bay leaves
3 or 4 carrots, thinly sliced
3 celery stalks, sliced
1 heaped tbsp tomato paste
½ tbsp cornstarch
8 sun-dried tomatoes, rehydrated (or from a jar in olive oil), chopped
a handful of cherry tomatoes
2 tbsp tamari
1 tbsp raw apple cider vinegar
1 cup veggie stock (see page 18 for homemade)
a large glass of red wine (or more stock)
1 (15-oz) can lima beans, drained and rinsed
2⅔ cups green or black pitted olives
freshly chopped parsley, to serve

In a large saucepan heat a glug of olive oil and cook the mushrooms for about 5 minutes on medium heat until they reduce in size and look golden. Put all the mushrooms in a bowl and set aside.

Add some more oil to the pan and gently cook the onion over medium heat, until softened. Add the garlic and all the herbs and after a minute or so add the carrots and celery. Cover with a lid and cook for 5 minutes.

Add the tomato paste and cornstarch, making sure you stir them in well. Now add the tomatoes, tamari, vinegar, stock, and wine, if using. Bring up to a simmer, then put a lid on the pan and cook on low for about 25 minutes. Add the beans and cooked mushrooms and cook for 15 minutes more. Stir in the olives and serve with lots of chopped parsley.

Keep portions of this in the freezer, defrost, and top with mashed potatoes for a hearty veggie shepherd's pie. Reheat in the oven at 400°F for 30 minutes.

MAKES 6 LARGE BURGERS | Prep time: 15 minutes, plus 30 minutes to chill | Cooking time: 1 hour

Smoky beet burgers with onion relish

These easy, earthy beet burgers can be made whatever size you like—larger patties for bigger appetites or mini-burgers for little ones. Beets are a fantastic mood booster, as they contain the compound betaine, which increases the production of serotonin. Quinoa adds extra protein, so these burgers are really well balanced. The burgers can be frozen, uncooked, for up to six weeks in an airtight container; defrost them in the fridge before cooking.

**For the onion relish
(or use a good-quality,
store-bought one)**
a glug of olive oil
2 small red onions,
  chopped
1 tbsp brown sugar
¼ cup red wine vinegar
4 cloves
a cinnamon stick

For the burgers
a glug of olive oil
1 small red onion, finely
  chopped
3½ oz mushrooms, finely
  chopped
sea salt and freshly ground
  black pepper
1 (15-oz) can kidney beans,
  drained and rinsed
½ cup precooked
  quinoa (or cook 3 tbsp
  dried quinoa according to
  the package instructions)
7 oz raw beets, grated
  (about 3 or 4 beets)
1 tsp smoked paprika
1 fresh chile, chopped
  (*optional*)
¾ cup plus 2 tbsp raw
  walnuts, crushed

To serve
6 burger buns, pitas, or wraps
salad

First make the onion relish. Heat some olive oil in
a saucepan and cook the red onions for 2 minutes.
Add the sugar and vinegar and simmer on low heat
for 15 minutes. Add the cloves and cinnamon stick
and cook, stirring regularly, until reduced to yummy
sticky relish. Remove the cloves and cinnamon stick
(if you can find them!) and set aside.

To make the burgers, heat a little oil in a large frying
pan over medium-low heat. Add the red onion and
cook until softened. Turn up the heat to medium and
add the mushrooms. Season with salt and pepper and
cook for 5 minutes. Remove from the heat and add
the beans. Mash, leaving some texture, then add the
quinoa, grated beets, paprika, chile (if using), and
walnuts, and mix thoroughly to combine.

With wet hands, form into whatever size burgers you
like. Cover and pop in the fridge for 30 minutes to
firm up (if you have time). Preheat the oven to 400°F.

Put the burgers on a baking sheet and cook in the
oven for 30 to 45 minutes, flipping over at the halfway
mark. Serve in a bun, pita, or a wrap with salad and
onion relish.

 *If you want to barbecue these burgers instead, precook in the oven for 20 minutes
and then pop on the barbecue for 5 minutes on each side.*

ALL NATURAL

Being in nature is one of the very best ways to de-stress and get yourself into a different headspace. There's nothing quite like it for helping you let go of whatever is crowding your mind and resetting your mood—or for blowing the cobwebs away, as my mum used to say! It is so good for us. And what's more, it's FREE! Just going for a walk in the park on your lunch break can give an enormous boost to your mood. Even if you don't live surrounded by woodlands and fields, there are plenty of ways to connect with nature daily.

Get outside every day

Can you walk or ride a bike to work instead of driving or taking the train? It may mean you have to get up a little earlier, but that dose of morning fresh air will make you feel alive and those endorphins will be buzzing. Maybe schedule any regular catch-up meetings outside instead of in a meeting room—find a bench and grab a coffee to go. (Use your own cup for added points with Mother Nature!) It's amazing how much more creative you can feel and how dynamics between people can also feel different.

Nature action plan

Maybe arrange a Sunday walk with friends, which can always be followed by a pub lunch as it's all about balance, right? Or change date night from your regular cinema trip to stargazing with a picnic or takeout. Get snuggled up under a blanket—it really is super special. Or simply chase your kids around a local park or beach. Even if it's cold, it doesn't matter; just wrap up and get outside for some free wholesome fun. Booking nature dates into your calendar will really help break up the same old routine.

Nature bathing

This idea is adapted from the Japanese art of forest bathing (*shinrin-yoku*). By committing to about ten minutes of sitting outdoors, you will begin to notice all the natural sounds around you—you will be amazed by just how much you can hear. Birds singing, bees buzzing, or just the sound of the wind in the trees—it is like going on a mini retreat and can really help you feel more centered. Nature is all around us—we just have to pay attention.

Begin or end your day with the sun

The sunset marks the ending of another day we have had the gift of, while a sunrise brings us the promise of a fresh start. It's one of those simple observations that gives me so much respect for the life we have been given. It is a good time to quietly rebalance and set some intentions.

joy

At times, self-care can start to feel a bit serious. Often, all you really need to do to help regain a sense of inner balance is simply to encourage a bit more joy into your life. Whether that's hanging out with friends, watching something funny on TV, or indulging in your favorite foods, it's all about pleasure and happiness, no strings attached.

I know, though, that if you're experiencing low moods or a lack of energy, it can feel hard to find joy. When you're feeling overwhelmed or anxious, happiness can be difficult to tap into, but sometimes just picking up the phone and ringing a good friend can help lift your mood. Or getting out of the house—ignoring that to-do list for half an hour—and going for a walk is enough to give you a boost. Start with small steps to reach those feelings of happiness again.

If joy is hard to come by right now, try one of these simple steps to help you find your way back to joy.

- **Go for a walk.** Maybe take a different route than usual. Look up and around you, rather than just down at the ground. Look at the sky, the trees; notice the different buildings above the shops. Changing where you place your focus can shift your whole perspective, too.

- **Make a bliss board.** Stick pictures and positive words that bring you joy to a piece of cardboard. Put it on your wall so you can see it every day.

- **Think of some nice things people have said about you,** or moments when you have felt real happiness and joy. Write them on pieces of paper and pop them in a jar. Pick one out to remind yourself of how great you are!

- **Smile at someone today.** Joy is contagious, so smile and it will make you and others glow and shine from the inside out.

- **Prepare some nourishing, colorful food.** The recipes in this section are simple and joyful, which I hope will put a great big smile your face.

Sunshine salad bowl

Eating colorful food cheers me up and makes me feel more alive. This sunshine salad does the job perfectly. Rainbow veggies and Moroccan spices, along with hearty chickpeas, make this a nourishing and satisfying salad for any time of year.

9 oz sweet potatoes,
  quartered (no need to peel)
1 (15-oz) can chickpeas,
  drained
olive oil
sea salt and freshly ground
  black pepper
2 tsp ras el hanout
  (a Moroccan spice)
10 to 15 cherry tomatoes,
  sliced
2 carrots, thinly sliced
2 small bell peppers,
  seeded and cut into chunks
2 small red onions, sliced
a handful of fresh mint,
  chopped
a handful of fresh cilantro,
  chopped
a small handful of chopped
  nuts (such as pistachios
  and hazelnuts), to serve

For the dressing
3 pitted dates, soaked in
  hot water for 5 minutes
  (save the water after)
7 tbsp extra-virgin olive oil
juice of 1 lemon
1 tsp mustard
¾-inch piece fresh ginger,
  peeled and chopped
½ tsp ground coriander
½ fresh chile, seeded and
  chopped
a pinch of ground cinnamon

Preheat the oven to 425°F. Line a baking sheet with parchment paper. Spread the sweet potatoes and chickpeas out on the lined sheet, drizzle with olive oil, and sprinkle with salt and pepper and the ras el hanout. Toss to coat, then cook for 25 to 30 minutes. Set aside to cool.

To make the dressing, blitz all the ingredients in a blender with 3 tbsp of the date soaking water, until smooth. If you'd like the dressing a bit thinner, add a little more of the soaking water and blend again.

Put all the other salad ingredients (except the nuts) in a serving bowl and mix together.

Add the cooled sweet potatoes and chickpeas and fold in the dressing. Scatter with the chopped nuts to serve.

Swap the sweet potatoes for cooked pasta.

Rainbow rolls

These multicolored raw rolls are guaranteed to bring you joy. They are perfect for tucking into a lunchbox to take to work to give your day a little midday rainbow magic. Of course, you can use any raw veggies you like. They're great to share with friends over, too—get everyone to roll their own!

1 carrot, thinly sliced
1 small yellow bell pepper, seeded and thinly sliced
1 small red bell pepper, seeded and thinly sliced
1 ripe mango, diced
1 beet, peeled and finely grated
½ cup cooked quinoa
a large bunch of mint, chopped
a large bunch of cilantro, chopped
1 tbsp alfalfa sprouts
8 spring roll rice paper wrappers

For the spicy, nutty dipping sauce

3 tbsp nut butter
1 tbsp tamari
2 tbsp maple syrup
juice of 1 lime
1 small fresh chile, chopped
½–inch piece of fresh ginger, peeled and grated
chopped parsley, for garnish (optional)

Get all the veggies, quinoa, and herbs prepped and ready. Boil roughly 2 cups water, pour it into a shallow bowl, and let it cool a little.

To make the dipping sauce, combine all the ingredients in a bowl and whisk together. If the sauce is too thick, add a little hot water to thin it out.

When ready to assemble the rolls, submerge a rice paper wrapper into the warm water for about 10 to 20 seconds to soften. Place it on a clean surface (not a wooden board) and gently smooth it out. Add some carrots, peppers, mango, beets, quinoa, and a small handful of herbs and alfalfa sprouts. Fold the bottom edge of the rice paper wrapper over the filling, then gently roll it over, folding in the sides to completely seal.

Place on a serving plate and cover with a damp clean kitchen towel to keep fresh. Repeat until all the rolls are made, then serve with the sauce to dip, garnished with a little extra chile and cilantro if you like.

Use brown rice instead of quinoa, or tortilla wraps instead of rice paper for a yummy rainbow wrap—perfect for a packed lunch!

Joyful banana cake

This is just the most joyful cake ever! Great for breakfast or to enjoy with a cuppa, it's a brilliant way for using up old bananas, too. Bananas are packed with vitamins and nutrients that can help lift our mood and assist in the production of our feel-good hormone serotonin.

4 ripe bananas, plus
  1 banana, sliced, for the topping
packed ¾ cup brown sugar
2 tbsp coconut oil, melted
5 tbsp almond milk (or any plant-based milk)
2 tsp vanilla extract
2¼ cups whole wheat flour
1 tsp baking powder
2 tsp ground cinnamon
1 tsp ground nutmeg
a pinch of sea salt
a small handful of pecans

Preheat the oven to 375°F. Line an 8-inch round cake pan with parchment paper.

In a large mixing bowl, mash the 4 bananas. Add the sugar, melted coconut oil, almond milk, and vanilla extract and whisk well. Add the flour, baking powder, spices, and salt and mix again.

Pour the cake batter into the lined pan, and top with the banana slices and pecans.

Bake for about 45 minutes, then cover with foil and bake for another 15 minutes, until a toothpick inserted into the middle of the cake comes out clean.

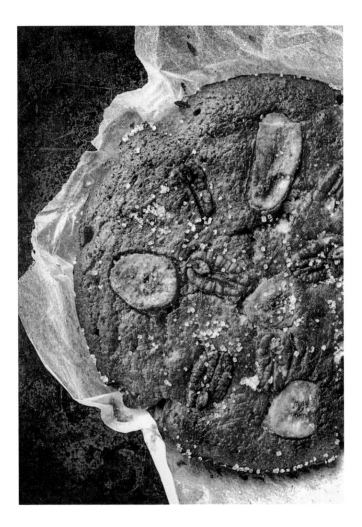

APPRECIATING THE SIMPLE THINGS

It's often the littlest things that can bring the most happiness. Start by writing a list of all the simple things that made you happy today. Here are mine:

- *Waking up in my warm, cozy bed*
- *Walking in the fresh air*
- *My loud and gorgeously funny children*
- *My dog*
- *Living by the sea*
- *Listening to music*

Try it, it's such a good practice to get into. None of these activities costs any money, but everything on this list made my heart glow and made me smile.

It's great to keep a list like this to one side for when you're feeling a bit down. You can go back to it and remember how these simple things have the power to change your mood. Looking back over lists like this really gives me a boost and cheers me up when I need it. Be mindful about enjoying the simple, but oh so special moments in your life, so they don't pass you by without your acknowledging them properly. Find meaning in the little things in life and really appreciate them.

Small gestures, like offering up your seat on a crowded bus to someone you think might need it or holding a door open for the people behind you, can really make a difference to someone else's day. Every single interaction you have with someone, no matter how small, is an opportunity to have a positive impact on both of your lives. Do something kind and see the ripple effect it can have.

Reflect

To reflect is simply to allow yourself the time and space to think. It's about giving yourself permission to question yourself in a positive way about your life and relationships and what your hopes are. It can be so easy to get caught up in day-to-day demands and forget to make space to really reflect on how you're feeling. Life can get stressful and all those little stresses can mount up and become a huge weight on your shoulders, but reflecting on them can help make things seem calmer and clearer. Sometimes, just by looking at a situation in a different light or from a different perspective, a solution to a problem may present itself or it may not feel as overwhelming as it once did.

Self-reflection has also really helped me understand more how I respond to certain situations. I have found ways to deal with circumstances more positively rather than letting them consume me. Being able to let things go if they don't serve us is an important act of self-care.

Taking time to reflect also provides the opportunity to practice gratitude for all that we have. When we feel weighed down and life feels hard, it can be difficult to feel grateful, but making space to explore these feelings can really improve how we feel. The process of taking time to reflect on where we are in our life can also help us develop a deeper understanding of what we may need to change, in order to grow and to create the life we want.

Previous chapters of this book have focused on building up your energies, restoring and nurturing your well-being physically and mentally, and regaining some equilibrium if you've been feeling out of balance. The following sections now encourage you to appreciate how far you have come and all you have to be proud of and grateful for. It's about being thankful and practicing kindness to who you are right now.

GROW SOMETHING

Nurturing a plant and appreciating it as it grows is a wonderful way to pause and reflect on life. By planting a seed, you are growing more than just something delicious to eat, you're growing gratitude.

Plant a few herb seeds in a pot on your windowsill or by the back door—basil, thyme, mint, or oregano are good ones to try—and when you sow them, or every time you water them, let your mind slow down and wander, reflecting on your day or your wider situation. It doesn't matter if it's an hour tending to your garden, or thirty seconds to smell your fresh herbs, revel in this precious moment to reflect on where you are and all you have to be grateful for. And that fresh herb salad you harvest will taste so much better because you grew it yourself.

light

Light is so important for our mood and well-being. When rays of light shine through, it helps us to see everything around us more clearly. When a surface is rough, light reflects from it in many different directions, just as when life gets tough, we may be uncertain of which direction to take. But, of course, those rays of light will also highlight exactly what it is that we need to see, as long as we take the time to pause and notice what is around us.

In the summer months, when light is in abundance, most people feel more energized. Those long evenings stretch out before us and we seem to be able to cram so much more into our days. At other times of the year, we may not have as much natural light as we want, waking up in the dark and coming home in the dark and working through those key hours of sunlight in the middle of the day.

It's natural to feel this ebb and flow and we shouldn't try to resist it as it's part of nature, but there are many ways to bring more light into our lives. Whether that's rejoicing in those balmy summer nights with long al fresco dinners, or creating cozy, candlelit moments during the winter months, celebrating the darkness outside with warmth inside and capturing the excitement this can bring.

When you can, try to really appreciate those moments of light. The recipes on the following pages are designed with that intention in mind—a lazy breakfast to enjoy as the sunshine streams through the window to wake you up, kebabs to barbecue with friends, and a light supper dish to enjoy over candlelight, enjoying the romance of a different kind of light.

Quinoa breakfast frittata

This easy baked egg-free frittata is perfect for a lazy breakfast or brunch. The protein from the quinoa and the iron in the greens provide an extra nutritional boost to start the day. This dish is also great cold with a salad for a packed lunch. The chickpea flour combined with water acts as a binder in the same way eggs do—you will be amazed at the results!

3 tbsp olive oil
5¼ oz mushrooms, finely chopped
1 small onion, finely chopped
1 small red bell pepper, seeded and finely chopped
3 garlic cloves, chopped
9 oz kale or spinach, stalks and ribs removed from the kale and chopped
1⅔ cups chickpea flour (gram flour)
sea salt and freshly ground black pepper
½ cup precooked quinoa (or cook 3 tbsp dried quinoa according to the package instructions)
a small bunch of parsley, chopped
mixed salad

Preheat the oven to 425°F. Line an 11-inch round cake pan with parchment paper.

In a large saucepan, warm half the olive oil over medium heat. Add the mushrooms, onion, and pepper and cook for about 5 minutes. Add the garlic and kale or spinach leaves, cook for 5 minutes, then remove from the heat and set aside.

In a large bowl, mix together the chickpea flour, the remaining olive oil, and 1½ cups water to make a batter. Season with a pinch of salt and pepper. Add the cooked vegetables, quinoa, and parsley, then stir until well combined.

Pour the mixture into the lined cake pan and bake for 25 minutes. Remove from the oven and leave to cool for 5 minutes, then slice into wedges.

Because the chickpea flour batter acts as a binder, you can make a scrambled egg-type dish. Cook some in vegan butter or olive oil in a nonstick frying pan on low heat, stirring constantly. Fold in some chopped chives and parsley and serve with a simple mixed salad.

Tofu skewers with peanut sauce

Cooking in nature can feel so liberating. These light and healthy kebabs are brilliant for a barbecue or cooked over a campfire. If the weather's not so good, though, they're just as delicious popped under the broiler, and even work in a pita pocket in a lunchbox. Tofu is a good plant-based source of protein and iron; it's vital that we include iron in our diet, as this helps reduce tiredness and aids better sleep. Serve with cooked brown rice or a big salad.

For the marinade

2 tbsp tamari
1 tbsp honey or maple syrup
½ tsp smoked paprika
½ tsp garlic powder
¾ cup peanut butter
7 tbsp coconut milk
juice of 2 limes
½ fresh chile, chopped

For the skewers

9 oz extra-firm tofu (I use chickpea tofu, but any firm tofu will do), cut into ¾-inch cubes
2 small bell peppers, seeded and cut into large chunks
1¾ oz button mushrooms, left whole
1 eggplant, cut into 1-inch chunks
2 small red onions, quartered
chopped fresh chile, to serve
cilantro leaves, to serve

In a shallow bowl, mix together all the ingredients for the marinade with 2 tablespoons water.

Add the tofu cubes and mix well to coat. Cover and leave for an hour or so in the fridge to marinate.

When ready to cook, alternate pieces of tofu and the veggies onto skewers. Broil or barbecue for 10 minutes on each side, brushing with the remaining marinade. The veggies should be cooked through and a little crispy around the edges.

Serve the kebabs scattered with the chopped chile and cilantro, and with any extra marinade as a sauce to drizzle on top.

These kebabs are also great made with pineapple chunks instead of tofu—although the pineapple won't provide the same iron and protein.

Caponata

This eggplant dish is so simple, but often simple is best! It makes the perfect light supper on its own, or serve it with rice or pasta. Eggplants are high in fiber so take care of the gut and digestive system. They also keep the heart healthy by naturally reducing high cholesterol.

olive oil
2 large eggplants, cut into
    ¾-inch chunks
2 tsp dried oregano
sea salt and freshly ground
    black pepper
1 small red onion, sliced
3 garlic cloves, chopped
1 (14.5-oz) can diced
    tomatoes
2 tbsp salted capers, rinsed
    and drained
2 tbsp raw apple cider
    vinegar
zest and juice of ½ lemon
toasted pine nuts (or
    almonds), to serve
finely chopped parsley,
    to garnish

In large saucepan, warm a good glug of olive oil over high heat. Add the eggplant and oregano, season with salt and pepper, and give it a good stir. Cook for 10 minutes, shaking the pan every now and then so it doesn't stick. When the eggplant is golden, add a little more oil along with the onion and garlic and cook for 2 minutes.

Stir in the tomatoes, capers, vinegar, and the lemon juice. Cook for about 15 minutes, until everything is soft and the sauce has reduced. Taste and season with more salt and pepper if you think it needs it. Serve warm or leave to cool, sprinkled with the pine nuts, some lemon zest, and chopped parsley.

 Add some sliced zucchini at the same time as the tomatoes to make it a more bountiful ratatouille-type dish.

CELEBRATE THE DARKNESS

As a child, I was scared of the dark, and so when I became a parent I remember thinking that I never wanted my kids to have that fear. I've tried to adopt a different approach to darkness. Instead of struggling with it and feeling negative about how it has made me feel in the past, I try to embrace it and celebrate what it can add to our lives.

When the light fades and we approach night, the darkness is a reminder that it's time to slow down. We need the darkness to rest and recharge for tomorrow, and it serves as a reminder for us to reflect on the day's events. The darkness of the winter months allows us to feel the same way about the year just gone. It asks us to slow down. To be still and to listen, to feel for what's around us, to tune into our body and get into the present.

Many people associate darkness with sadness or "dark times" in their lives. But emotional darkness can also be used as a source of wisdom. When life is tough and we are feeling hurt or broken, it can be tempting to scramble over our feelings or brush them under the carpet. We try and get back to "normal"—or into the "light"— as quickly as we can. But if we actually pause and feel our true feelings, we may learn something from that moment of darkness. It may even point us toward what we really want. Being able to sit with uncomfortable thoughts takes a lot of courage, but it also teaches us that we are brave, and when we come through to the other side (because we will) we will have light again!

Having a few rituals to honor the wonder of darkness can bring joy and excitement to something that so many people try to avoid. Something as simple as having a candlelit dinner to celebrate just how gorgeous and cozy these times are can really change your feelings toward the dark. Or how about 4 p.m. tea and biscuits by candlelight in the depth of winter?

harvest

Traditionally, harvest time marks a pause in the cycle of the year to celebrate the bountiful harvest collected. It is about being grateful for crops safely gathered in, and it is about sharing that food with others. It's an opportunity to celebrate and be thankful for those who planted it, nurtured it, and harvested it.

I love this mindful thinking, which can often get lost in our busy lives. Just taking a moment to really consider where the food on my plate has come from helps me to appreciate how lucky I am. Thinking like this throughout the year creates little moments for us to feel grateful for those small things in life that we often take for granted. It also provides a chance for us to reflect on how we might make some subtle changes in order to live and eat more sustainably, using produce grown near to us or by supporting our local community.

The idea of harvest time is also about showing thanks for the abundance and happiness we have, perhaps even saying it out loud or writing it down to affirm it. It's a time to reflect on what we have planted in our own lives, because this is what we will reap in our personal harvest later. Be sure to plant new ideas and positive habits that make you feel good and strong and happy. Nurture them carefully, so that when you harvest them you will be sure to see the benefits. Say goodbye to any old habits you don't need anymore and that you definitely don't want to see in your harvest!

The recipes in this section celebrate the richness of our wonderful produce. They are colorful dishes, full of positivity and life to inspire those feelings in yourself, too.

Eat-the-rainbow salad

Something as simple as a fresh, colorful salad can give you a real boost of energy and make you feel full of life. I love that this salad contains all the colors of the rainbow—but please feel free to add any extras to make it even more abundant! If you grow your own veggies or herbs (see page 95), this is the perfect way to show them off, or get down to your local market and see what they have on offer. The dressing is packed with flavor and makes this an extra-special celebration of veg. Add some edible flowers if you like, to make it look really pretty!

For the ginger dressing
1-inch piece of fresh ginger, peeled and chopped
3 tbsp tahini
2 tbsp maple syrup
1 tbsp miso paste
2 tbsp raw apple cider vinegar
1 tbsp tamari

For the salad
2 small sweet potatoes, diced
1 small broccoli, chopped into florets
3½ cups baby kale
3⅓ cups spinach
½ small red cabbage, finely chopped
2 carrots, grated
1¼ cups walnuts
1 small avocado, chopped

To make the ginger dressing, put all the ingredients in a lidded jar with a splash of water and give it a really good shake. (You can also whisk it together in a small bowl.)

Bring a saucepan of water to a boil and steam the sweet potatoes in a steamer basket for 12 minutes. Add the broccoli and steam for 3 to 5 minutes, until just tender. Put both aside to cool.

To assemble, combine the cooled sweet potatoes and broccoli in a large serving bowl and add the kale, spinach, cabbage, carrots, walnuts, and avocado. Pour the dressing over top and toss to coat.

 For extra sweetness you could add some chopped fruit, such as apples or oranges, or dried fruit like raisins.

SERVES 4 | Prep time: 15 minutes | Cooking time: 40 minutes

Pumpkin and chickpea stew

This nourishing stew is great if you're feeling a bit run down or under the weather. It's so warming and wholesome, with a little kick from the ginger and paprika. Pumpkins are a great source of potassium, which helps boost your mood. Low levels of potassium can cause irritability, chronic pain, and fatigue. I used to make this dish weekly when we lived in Barcelona, as we lived next to the famous food market La Boqueria, which sells wonderful pumpkins and squashes in autumn. Serve it on its own or with rice or quinoa.

a glug of olive oil
1 small onion, chopped
1 celery stalk, finely
  chopped
2 carrots, chopped into
  small chunks
2 garlic cloves, chopped
½-inch piece of fresh ginger,
  peeled and chopped
1 tsp ground ginger
2 tsp smoked paprika
1 bell pepper, seeded and
  chopped
5¼ oz sweet potato,
  chopped (no need to peel)
1 small cooking pumpkin or
  winter squash, peeled
  and chopped into chunks
  (about 14 oz peeled
  weight)
1 tomato, chopped
2 tbsp tomato paste
1 (15-oz) can chickpeas,
  drained and rinsed
2 cups veggie stock (see
  page 18 for homemade)
sea salt and freshly ground
  black pepper
a bunch of parsley,
  chopped
1⅔ cups spinach, chopped,
  to serve
2 tbsp chopped, toasted
  nuts of choice
lemon wedges, to serve

In a large saucepan, heat the olive oil over medium heat and cook the onion until softened.

Add the celery, carrots, garlic, fresh and ground ginger, and the paprika and cook for 5 minutes. Add the bell pepper, sweet potato, pumpkin, tomato, tomato paste, chickpeas, stock, and some salt and pepper. Bring to a boil, cover with a lid, decrease the heat to low, and simmer for 30 minutes, or until the pumpkin is soft but not mushy.

Stir in the parsley until wilted and season with more salt and pepper to taste.

Serve with the chopped spinach and top with toasted nuts and a squeeze of lemon juice.

Blend any leftovers with a 13.5-oz can of coconut milk to make a thick hearty soup, which can also be frozen.

Harvest crumble

Who doesn't love a crumble? It's the ultimate in comfort food. This healthier version uses oats and nuts for a delicious crunchy topping, which adds even more flavor. Berries and apples will give you a brilliant vitamin boost. If fresh berries aren't in season you can use frozen berries, and you can swap blackberries for any other berry you fancy. This is also great for breakfast with a little fresh fruit added—it's like a granola pot. And, hey, who doesn't like eating dessert for breakfast?

For the filling
4 medium apples (any type), peeled and diced
1½ cups fresh or frozen blackberries
packed ¼ cup brown sugar
1 tsp ground cinnamon
1 tbsp lemon juice
2 cloves

For the topping
1⅔ cups rolled oats
1 tsp ground cinnamon
3 tbsp brown or coconut sugar
1½ cups pecans, walnuts, or almonds (or a combination)
6 pitted dates
1 tbsp coconut oil
2 tbsp shredded coconut

To serve
plant-based ice cream or yogurt

Place all the ingredients for the filling in a saucepan with 2 tablespoons water. Bring to a boil over high heat, stirring, then turn the heat down to low and cook for another 10 minutes, until the apples are soft. Remove from the heat and set aside.

Preheat the oven to 400°F.

To make the topping, put all the ingredients in a food processor and pulse until well combined. If you don't have a food processor, chop the nuts and dates roughly and use your hands to mix them together with the other ingredients in a large bowl until you have a crumbly consistency.

Spoon the fruit filling into a deep 9-inch pie dish and top with the crumble. Bake for about 20 minutes, until the top is golden and you can see the fruit bubbling away underneath. Serve with plant-based ice cream or yogurt.

 Swap apples for pears, and blackberries for raspberries, for a twist on the classic.

BE GRATEFUL

This is probably one of the most important lessons I have learned. When I became open to understanding what it really meant, almost instantly everything became so much better. I strongly believe that practicing being grateful has the power to block out negative emotions. You can't really pay attention to what's missing or what's not going well in your life if you let your mind focus only on the good things. By focusing on all the good, those feelings and situations that aren't serving us will start to feel like they are dropping away.

How to be grateful

Start by giving thanks for the small things that have happened today. For instance, it might be that you woke up in a warm bed or that the sun is shining. How does it make you feel when you show gratitude for these little things? Write your feelings down and hold on to that positive emotion. You may even want to start keeping a gratitude journal specifically to capture these thoughts, jotting down five things every day that you are grateful for. Focusing on the positive will make a huge difference to how you feel.

Once you start to become more aware of the little things that bring you gratitude, practice appreciating them as they happen. Try and get into the habit of being present, right now, and not always wishing for something you may have had in the past or longing for the future. Being grateful for what is happening in the moment will help you develop a happier and more positive outlook.

Even when it's hard (because I know it can be: I'm not saying jump for joy every day because life's not like that), try to find something positive out of your situation.

Don't forget to share the love! Include others in your expressions of feeling grateful. Why don't you write a friend or loved one a gratitude letter? Or you could share what you're grateful for today with the rest of the family as you eat dinner together. Taking time to acknowledge the good stuff means you're much less likely to waste time moaning about the negative, and you'll be giving off pure positive vibes.

feast

To feast is a luxury that we most often associate with celebrations. I don't think there is anything more wonderful than cooking up a feast and sharing it with friends and family. This sounds very decadent and indulgent, but it doesn't have to be lavish. It can be done on a budget, and you can share the load so it is manageable and stress free. Gathering the people you love around the table lets you feast, not only on delicious food, but also on the joy, laughter, and happiness that being together brings.

At other times, though, I love to prepare a meal just for myself, so that I can feast alone. Make yourself a special dish because you deserve it. Enjoy every mouthful and feast on the peace and quiet and the stillness around you.

I also love the concept of feasting with your eyes—they say we eat first with our eyes and I truly believe this. Making your food look good doesn't have to be complicated. Simply using brightly colored veggies and fruits in your cooking, and maybe decorating the food with a few freshly snipped herbs or even a couple of edible flowers, can really make a dish look beautiful and inviting.

A NO-STRESS GUIDE TO
"HOW TO FEAST WITH YOUR FRIENDS"

- **Ask your guests to each bring a dish that has a special meaning to them.**
  I love this idea, as it will make your feast vibrant and different and your friends'
  personalities will show through in their chosen dish.

- **Make some pretty napkins out of colorful material.** You have probably got odd
  bits stashed somewhere! It looks great when they are mismatched, too. Just cut
  squares and tie with string.

- **Pick up some vases from thrift shops** and arrange some flowers and fresh herbs
  in them.

- **Swap seats after each course** so you get to chat to someone different throughout
  the night.

- **Choose a dish you can prepare in advance** so you're not stressing when your
  friends arrive (my Jackfruit Taco Party, page 64, Curry Feast in this section on page
  120, and the Down-to-Earth One-Pot Stew on page 76 are great suggestions!).

- **Clean up as you go along** so you're not left with a pile of plates as high as the Eiffel
  Tower to wash at the end of the night. And ask someone to help you—it can often
  be when good chats happen.

- **Cook using a new ingredient**—it can be a great conversation starter.

- **Invite someone who may need some extra love and support at the moment**—
  it's such a lovely feeling when you're down and a friend reaches out.

- **Get another date in for a few months' time so you have something to look
  forward to.** Take turns hosting so you can share the responsibility.

Roasted golden quinoa pilaf

A beautiful fruity pilaf made with protein-rich quinoa instead of rice. The chestnuts are high in folic acid and are packed with B vitamins, which support brain function. The dried nuts and fruit add wonderful flavor and jewel-like colors, as well as a boost to vitamin and protein levels. This dish is lovely served with a spoonful of plant-based natural yogurt.

a glug of olive oil
1 small onion, chopped
2 garlic cloves, chopped
5¼ oz butternut squash,
  peeled and cut into small
  chunks
5¼ oz button mushrooms,
  sliced
7 oz vacuum-packed
  chestnuts, chopped
½ cup plus 1 tbsp quinoa
2 tsp sweet smoked paprika
2 tsp dried oregano
2 tbsp tamari
2 cups veggie stock (see
  page 18 for homemade)
sea salt and freshly ground
  black pepper
zest and juice of 1 lemon
a bunch of parsley, finely
  chopped
¾ cup plus 2 tbsp dried
cranberries
¾ cup dried apricots,
  chopped
1¼ cups mixed nuts (such as
  walnuts, cashews,
  hazelnuts, and Brazil
  nuts), chopped

Heat some olive oil in a large frying pan set over medium heat. Add the onion, garlic, and squash and cook for 5 to 10 minutes, until the onion is soft and the squash has a little bit of color.

Add the mushrooms and cook for a couple of minutes, until golden brown, then add the chestnuts, quinoa, paprika, oregano, tamari, and stock. Season well with salt and pepper, and simmer for 15 minutes, until the veggies and quinoa are soft.

Remove the pan from the heat and stir in the lemon zest and juice and the parsley, dried fruit, and nuts.

 This is a great mixture to stuff veggies with, such as large portobello mushrooms or bell peppers. Keep any extra—it will freeze in an airtight container for up to 6 weeks.

Curry feast

My favorite feast of all has to be a curry one. I absolutely love cooking curries, and my pantry is full to bursting with little colorful jars of spices. The cauliflower provides some powerful health benefits. It's packed with nutrients and contains unique antioxidants that may reduce inflammation—in particular choline, which supports brain function. The apple chutney adds some real tang and makes this dish feel really special, but you can use a good store-bought alternative if you don't have time to make your own. Add more fresh chile if you like it hotter!

For the spicy apple chutney

4 small onions, chopped
2 lb 4 oz apples, peeled, cored, and chopped
⅔ cup golden or Thompson seedless raisins
2 tsp ground coriander
2 tsp chile powder
2 tsp pumpkin pie spice blend
3 cloves
a pinch of sea salt
packed 1⅔ cups brown sugar
7 tbsp raw apple cider vinegar

For the curry

2¼ cups brown rice
1 tbsp coconut oil
1 tsp cumin seeds
2 tsp mustard seeds
2 garlic cloves, chopped
1-inch piece of fresh ginger, peeled and chopped
1 small onion, chopped
1 tbsp curry powder
1 tbsp garam masala
1 tbsp chile powder
2 tsp ground cinnamon
1 (14.5-oz) can diced tomatoes
1 (15-oz) can chickpeas, rinsed and drained
5 cups spinach, chopped
¼ cauliflower, in florets
chopped fresh chile and cilantro, to serve

To make the apple chutney, put all the chutney ingredients in a pan and slowly bring to a boil, until the sugar has dissolved. Simmer for about 1 hour, stirring from time to time to prevent the chutney from sticking to the pan. When it is nice and thick, the chutney is ready. Keep in a sealed, sterilized jar in the fridge for up to 2 months.

For the curry, first cook the rice in a saucepan of boiling water for 20 to 25 minutes.

Meanwhile, heat the coconut oil in a frying pan over medium heat. Cook the cumin and mustard seeds until they start to pop, then add the garlic, ginger, and onion and cook for 5 minutes, until the onion is softened.

Stir in the curry powder, garam masala, chile powder, and cinnamon. When the onion is completely coated in the spicy oil, add the tomatoes and chickpeas and mix together. Pour in ¾ cup plus 2 tbsp water, turn up the heat, and simmer for 2 minutes.

Add a handful of the spinach and stir until wilted. Repeat until all of the spinach is used. Add the cauliflower florets to the pan and stir to combine. Lower the heat and simmer for 8 to 10 minutes, stirring occasionally. Serve the curry with the rice, chopped fresh chile and cilantro, and some apple chutney.

 Top with some sliced banana for some additional mood-boosting properties and extra sweetness. Try making this with sweet potato instead of cauliflower.

Pretty pineapple dessert

Oh, so simple but, oh, so good! Pineapples scream sunshine and boost our serotonin levels, which help us feel happy. They are also packed with vitamin C, which is good for our immune system. This dessert is perfect for a barbecue with friends on a hot summer night. If you like things with a kick, add a few chile flakes. Serve this treat on its own or with berries and/or plant-based ice cream.

1 pineapple, cored, cut in half lengthwise, and sliced into equal-size pieces
2 tsp ground cinnamon
2 tbsp coconut oil, melted
2 tbsp brown sugar
plant-based ice cream, mixed berries, and/or pomegranate seeds, to serve (*optional*)
basil leaves, to garnish
chopped hazelnuts, to garnish

Arrange the pineapple pieces on a baking sheet. Sprinkle lightly with 1 tsp of the cinnamon. Mix together the coconut oil, brown sugar, and the remaining 1 tsp cinnamon and spread on top of the pineapple.

Preheat the broiler or grill. Broil or barbecue for about 10 minutes or until the pineapple is golden brown. Serve with the plant-based ice cream, mixed berries, and/or pomegranate seeds, as desired, and garnish with the basil leaves and chopped hazelnuts.

 Swap the pineapple for peaches or nectarines.

SHARE THE FEAST

Feasting is also a time for sharing with others. Not only in the literal sense, with friends and family, but also for sharing our luck and love with those who need it most. Giving something back to others is so important—and it can actually benefit our own mental health, too.

I have always tried to be involved with helping my community in some way or another. When I lived in Barcelona, I was a part of a weekly soup run for the homeless and used to make a huge pot of veggie and lentil soup to be collected and shared out. It cost just a few dollars to make and just a little bit of my time, but what I gained from doing it was so rich and fulfilling. Explaining to the kids why we were making the soup, and how it was going to help others, was an important lesson for them, and it became a family ritual where we would all help and work together to share our feast!

In Brighton, I now raise money for a local charity, the Brighton Dolphin Project, which helps look after the sea life and keep the beaches clean. It has opened up new connections with my community, I've developed new friendships, and it is helping a cause close to my heart.

It's often said that it is better to give than receive and I really believe this. By putting other people's needs before our own, we can boost our mood, feel grateful for what we have, and boost our own confidence and self-esteem. Even simple daily good deeds can make a difference. Random acts of kindness and sharing your love around will just make the world a better place.

Ways you can get involved with helping your local community:

- Volunteer in a local thrift shop
- Cook for a soup kitchen
- Join a befriending service for the elderly
- Help at an animal rescue center or sanctuary
- Donate food and sanitary products to your local food bank
- Get involved in a beach or park cleanup to reduce plastic, waste, and litter
- Help your neighbors
- Give someone a smile (try it, it's contagious!)

When we help others, we feel happier and calmer. It distracts us from our own problems for a bit while we engage in a meaningful and selfless act. I've also found that when you get involved in the local community, it really makes you feel like you belong. If you are feeling lonely, it gives you a sense of togetherness and helps you feel less isolated.

Choose something that you enjoy doing, as it will come easier and feel more like a pleasure. Don't overdo it, though, by saying yes to too much. You must consider your needs, too.

Every now and then, it can feel as though life needs a bit of a shake-up.
We might already know we need to make a specific change, or maybe we just
feel like we've lost a bit of our mojo and need to get some of our old energy
and vitality back.

If you're not sure where to begin, a good place to start is by looking at what it
is you want to see in your new life. And what you will need to say goodbye to
in order to make room for those changes. We can often feel held back by not
being able to let go of the past and the fear we associate with the unknown.
But why don't we start to look at this in a different way and be excited for the
unknown and believe we deserve what we need to be happy?

Look at your current thought patterns and daily actions. Are they in line with
what you want? We generally wake up at the same time most mornings and
follow the same routines as we do every day, but if we do the same thing day
after day in exactly the same way, how can we expect to manifest any change?

Take small steps at first. Maybe it's picking out what you're going to wear
the night before so you don't feel rushed in the morning. Or walking to work
instead of driving so you can get some fresh air and avoid the stress of rush
hour traffic. Or trying out a new recipe or ingredient tonight! Even these little
changes can have an immediate impact, and once you see the difference even
small changes can make you'll feel inspired to make even more changes.

Remember that small steps lead us to where we want to be. You are the one
who is in control, so go for it. Embrace the new and let go of the fear of the
unknown so you can bring more energy and vitality into your life. Know that
you have the potential to make it all happen. You have every tool inside you to
make those changes.

energy

When we're feeling low on energy, the first things we usually think about doing are getting more sleep, eating well, and doing some regular exercise. These are, of course, all essential to good health and well-being, but by focusing only on these we can be at risk of ignoring any emotional stress or worry that could be zapping our energies, too.

In order to get those energy levels up again it's important to take a more holistic approach. Look at all the different areas of your life and see if you can identify anything that is draining you physically or emotionally. As far as is possible, look for ways to reduce—or preferably get rid of completely— anything that is wasting your energy.

Looking after your emotional well-being is just as important as caring for your physical health. The recipes in this section have been chosen especially with boosting energy levels in mind, and using ingredients to keep blood sugar levels stable. This will help avoid those peaks and crashes that can lead to low moods and tiredness.

START HERE

MORNING
SUN SALUTATION
FOR ENERGY

ENERGY BALLS, 5 WAYS

Energy balls are a wonderful anytime snack made from natural ingredients, such as dried fruits and nuts. Here is a basic energy ball mix followed by five different flavor combinations, but play around with the recipes according to your own tastes. I have used walnuts and dates as the base mix, but you can easily change the nuts to almonds, cashews, or raw peanuts and the dates to dried apricots or dried figs. The balls will keep for up to six weeks in the freezer and only take a few minutes to defrost, so make a big batch to keep on hand for whenever you need an instant pick-me-up.

Basic energy ball mix

¾ cup plus 2 tbsp walnuts
mounded 1 cup pitted dates, soaked in hot
  water for 5 minutes (save the water after
  soaking)
1 tbsp coconut oil
1 tbsp rolled oats
1 tbsp maple syrup or honey

Place the nuts in a food processor and blitz for 30 seconds. Add the dates and pulse for 30 seconds, then add the oil, oats, and maple syrup and blend for 2 minutes. You may need to add a little of the date water if the mixture is very thick. (If you don't have a food processor, you can use a blender, loosening the mixture with a little warm water, if necessary.)

Now add your choice of flavors—see list—or leave plain. Blend for another minute and then roll into even-size balls, about 1 inch in diameter.

Decorate by rolling the balls through a little coconut or some seeds, if you like. Keep in an airtight container in the fridge for up to 1 week, or in the freezer for up to 6 weeks.

• CACAO AND COCONUT
Packed with essential fatty acids and magnesium, this is a fab mood booster.

¼ cup shredded or flaked coconut
2 tbsp cacao powder

• HEMP AND CHIA SEED
Extra protein and fiber, and essential amino acids to help relieve anxiety.

2 tbsp hemp hearts
1 tbsp chia seeds

• SPIRULINA & CHOPPED NUTS
Great for before exercise and will help with concentration.

2 tbsp chopped nuts, plus more to decorate
2 tsp spirulina

• MOCHA
The ultimate mid-morning pick-me-up.

2 tsp ground coffee
1 tbsp cacao powder

• BEET
Beet powder is rich in antioxidants and nutrients to reduce tiredness.

1 tbsp beet powder, plus extra for coating

Rich ragù

This simple, rich tomato ragù is delicious served with any type of pasta or veggie noodles, such as butternut squash or zucchini. Adding spinach ups the vitamins and iron to help combat tiredness. The walnuts provide extra protein and energy, as well as the wonderful mood-boosting mineral selenium, which helps reduce anxiety and sets off those happy hormones.

olive oil
½ small onion, finely chopped
4 garlic cloves, chopped
1 (14.5 oz) can diced tomatoes
a few sun-dried tomatoes, rehydrated (or from a jar in olive oil), chopped
1 tsp brown sugar
2 tsp dried oregano
a bunch of basil
sea salt and freshly ground black pepper
10½ oz pasta, or veggie noodles
5 cups spinach, chopped
1¾ cups walnuts, chopped
freshly chopped parsley, to serve

Heat some olive oil in a large saucepan and cook the onion and garlic on medium heat for about 5 minutes, until softened and slightly translucent. Add the diced tomatoes, sun-dried tomatoes, brown sugar, oregano, and most of the basil, reserving a few basil leaves to serve, and season with salt and pepper. Simmer for 10 minutes, until slightly reduced.

If you are serving this with pasta, prepare it while the sauce is reducing. Cook the pasta about 2 minutes shy of the package instructions. Drain and set aside.

Blitz the sauce with an immersion blender until smooth, if desired (or you can just leave it chunky).

Stir the spinach and walnuts into the sauce. Add the cooked pasta to the pan and toss to coat with the sauce. (If you are using veggie noodles, simply fold them into the sauce and warm through for a couple of minutes.) Garnish with the reserved basil leaves and the parsley.

 For extra decadence, drizzle with pesto (see the recipe on page 18). This ragù can also be used as an excellent base for a pizza, or be spread on toast for a quick snack.

Roasted cauliflower and lentil bowl

This wonderful hearty salad is perfect for a lunch—hot or cold—or as a side, maybe with the Curry Feast on page 120. Nutrient-packed, the lentils give you energy along with folate and iron, which assist in regulating sleep patterns. The antioxidant-rich greens naturally aid detoxing to give your liver a cleanse.

2⅔ cups French lentils
5 carrots, quartered
  lengthwise
½ cauliflower, cut into
  florets
3⅓ cups mustard greens (or
  any leafy greens),
  chopped
3½ cups baby kale

For the mustard dressing
1 tbsp mustard seeds
2 garlic cloves, chopped
¼ cup plus 1 tbsp olive oil
1 tbsp honey
¼ cup plus 3 tbsp raw apple
  cider vinegar
zest and juice of 2 lemons

To massage the greens
3 tbsp olive oil
a pinch of sea salt

To serve
1 fresh chile, chopped
freshly chopped parsley

Cook the lentils in a pot of boiling water for 30 minutes, until tender. Drain and set aside.

Preheat the oven to 400°F. Line a baking sheet with parchment paper.

To make the mustard dressing, blitz all the ingredients in a small blender, or use a mortar and pestle to grind the seeds before mixing everything together well with a spoon.

Put the carrots and cauliflower on the lined baking sheet and coat well with half of the mustard dressing. Roast for 20 minutes until soft in the middle and nicely roasted around the edges.

Meanwhile, combine the mustard greens and baby kale in a large serving bowl with the olive oil and salt. Massage with your hands for a couple of minutes (this makes the greens easier to digest), until the greens are well coated.

Add the carrots and cauliflower to the bowl with the greens. Serve with the rest of the mustard dressing drizzled over the top, scatter with the chopped chile and parsley.

 If you have any leftovers, warm them up with a teaspoon of curry powder and serve with cooked rice and a spoonful of mango chutney.

Energizing green stir-fry

A simple, quick dish that is perfect for lunch or a light supper—it's a great one to take cold to work in a lunchbox, too. In-season new potatoes taste sweet and delicious, and their carb content will give you a real energy boost.

14 oz new potatoes, halved
a glug of olive oil
½ small onion, chopped
2 garlic cloves, chopped
½ fresh chile, chopped
¾ cup capers, drained and rinsed
12 asparagus spears, woody ends removed
6⅔ cups spinach, chopped
7 oz kale, stalks and ribs removed, chopped
a bunch of parsley, chopped
sea salt and freshly ground black pepper
zest and juice of 1 lemon

Cook the potatoes in a large pot of boiling water for 15 minutes, until tender. Drain well.

Heat the olive oil in a large frying pan and cook the onion and garlic for about 5 minutes, until softened and slightly translucent.

Add the drained potatoes, chile, capers, asparagus, spinach, and kale and cook for another 5 minutes. Stir in the chopped parsley. Season really well with salt and pepper, and serve with a squeeze of lemon juice and the zest over the top.

 Swap new potatoes for cooked baby beets. They give it an amazing flavor and incredible color!

CREATIVITY FOR ENERGY

Taking yourself out of your regular routine and trying activities that encourage creativity are great ways to boost your energy levels. Thinking creatively can also give you a new perspective on life. Try these simple ways to get those creative juices flowing!

Make a vision board

A vision board is a powerful tool that can really help you focus on what you want for the future. Choosing what to put on your vision board can be very revealing. Write down your wishes and dreams, then go through some magazines and cut out words or pictures that represent them. Stick them to a piece of cardboard and look at it daily to reaffirm your intentions.

Rearrange your furniture

Rearranging a room can make you feel excited about your environment again. I'm not talking about redecorating here, simply moving the furniture or even just the pictures on the walls. At the same time, get rid of any clutter and items that don't give off a happy vibe!

Plant some flowers

Even if you live in an apartment like I do, you can still flex those green fingers! Plant up some pots on the balcony or a windowsill. Being around nature can be revitalizing and mood-enhancing (see page 95). And there's nothing like that feeling of accomplishment once those little plants start to grow!

Go through your music collection

This has to be one of my favorite things to do when I need an energy boost or am feeling a bit low. There is nothing like your beloved old tunes to lift the spirits. I love nothing more than turning the volume up and dancing over breakfast while my kids laugh at me in despair.

Explore the unknown

The same old routine and habits can make us feel claustrophobic and quash our creativity. Step out of your comfort zone for a moment and face any fears you may have. You will feel liberated and energized.

new beginnings

The prospect of starting over or beginning something new can feel tough and more than a little daunting, but if you flip it over and see it from the other side, it can also be an exciting time for opportunities and growth.

Without new beginnings, we can get stuck in the past or in our old bad habits. It's really important to make changes happen and to not be scared of what's around that corner.

All those things you've been dreaming about—the goals you have written on your bucket lists, the ideas that are in your head (or on your vision board!)—but that you never thought would actually happen, really can happen if you start to believe in them.

It's not good for us to hang on to the past; it can be so draining to keep going over all those old feelings. Let go of all the things that you can't control and hold on tight to all the good things you have in your life today. Appreciate what you have learned along the way to get to where you are now, and embrace what is to come.

The recipes in this section will fuel your mind as well as your body with lightness and excitement, which is what you need when facing new challenges. They will give you a lift and a boost, to give you the strength to master any new beginnings and power you through any tough decisions you need to make.

Panzanella

If you've never made panzanella before, I encourage you to give it a go. The flavors are intense and vibrant—just how we should be feeling as we head into a new start! It's also a great way to use up leftover bread. Beets give it an amazing color, while also being full of minerals and antioxidants.

For the dressing
3 tbsp red wine vinegar
½ cup plus 2 tbsp olive oil
2 garlic cloves, chopped
1 tsp honey

For the panzanella
1 small loaf of day-old
 rustic bread (about
 14 oz), cut or torn into
 1-inch pieces
extra-virgin olive oil
sea salt
1¾ lb tomatoes, cut into
 large chunks
1 cucumber, halved
 lengthwise, chopped
1 (15-oz) can white beans
 (or any canned beans),
 drained and rinsed
4 beets, cooked and
 quartered (from a jar if
 you can't get fresh)
8 small radishes, quartered
a small bunch of basil,
 leaves only
freshly ground black pepper

First, make the dressing by blitzing all the ingredients in a small blender until smooth, or shake together in a lidded jar.

Toss the bread pieces with 2 tablespoons olive oil and season with salt. Toast in a medium skillet over medium heat for 5 to 10 minutes, until golden, turning the pieces over halfway through. Set aside.

Combine the tomatoes, cucumber, beans, beets, radishes, and basil leaves in a bowl. Add the toasted bread and drizzle the dressing over the top. Season with pepper and more salt, if desired, and eat straightaway.

 You can use any canned beans, but I like lima beans because they are extra creamy.

SERVES 4 | Prep time: 15 minutes | Cooking time: 40 minutes

Green goddess risotto

Leeks and peas are wonderfully sweet, and I've also used asparagus here, which, when it is in season, is the most perfect celebration of spring. If you can't find it, use green beans instead. Brown rice contains more fiber than white rice, leaving you feeling fuller and providing a longer release of energy. It's also very calming, which is helpful if you are facing big decisions.

For the risotto

2 tbsp olive oil
½ small onion, chopped
2 garlic cloves, chopped
1 small leek, sliced
¾ cup Arborio or Carnaroli rice or short-grain brown rice
1¾ cups veggie stock (see page 18 for homemade)
a small bunch of asparagus, woody ends removed, cut into 1-inch pieces (or long green beans if asparagus isn't in season)
1¼ cups snow peas or sugar snap peas
⅔ cup frozen peas
a small glass of dry white wine (or add more stock)
sea salt and freshly ground black pepper
1 tbsp tamari
1 tbsp raw apple cider vinegar
freshly chopped parsley, to serve
lemon wedges, to serve

For the cashew Parmesan *(optional)*

1 cup raw unsalted cashews
1½ tbsp nutritional yeast
½ tsp onion powder
½ tsp garlic powder
a pinch of sea salt

Heat the olive oil in a large saucepan over medium heat. Add the onion, garlic, and leek and cook for 5 minutes, until the onion is soft. Stir in the rice to coat in the oil.

Pour in half the stock and cook, stirring constantly, until the liquid is almost completely absorbed. Decrease the heat to a simmer. Keep adding the stock, a ladleful at a time, stirring until it has all been absorbed and the rice is just tender. This should take about 25 minutes. You may need to add more liquid; if so, add a little water.

While the risotto cooks, make the cashew Parmesan, if using. Place all the ingredients in a blender and blitz until it resembles a coarse powder.

When the rice is al dente and most of the liquid has been absorbed, stir the veggies into the rice and add the wine or extra stock. Cook for 3 minutes or so, then season really well with salt and pepper, and stir in the tamari and apple cider vinegar.

Serve in bowls with lots of chopped parsley, a wedge of lemon, and a sprinkle of the cashew Parmesan.

 This is absolutely delicious served cold as a rice salad the next day. Add some more chopped herbs and a squeeze of lemon to freshen it up.

Berry chia pudding

Such a simple but super-tasty and satisfying pudding. Chia seeds are a great source of protein, too. The fruits give it a gorgeous color—you can add any fruits you like to this, the more the better! Make it even prettier with a few edible flowers.

⅔ cup chia seeds
1⅔ cups coconut milk (or any plant-based milk)
1 vanilla pod, halved lengthwise and seeds scraped (or use 1 tsp vanilla extract)
2 tbsp maple syrup
1¼ cups fresh or frozen berries (such as strawberries and/or blueberries), defrosted if frozen, chopped
a little grated vegan chocolate (*optional*)
2 tbsp toasted coconut flakes
edible flowers (*optional*)

The night before
In a bowl or individual jars, mix the chia seeds with the coconut milk, vanilla, and maple syrup. Cover and chill in the fridge.

The next day
Serve topped with berries, grated vegan chocolate if using, and coconut flakes. Decorate with edible flowers, if you like.

 This makes a wonderful breakfast, too. Add granola and more fruit for a nourishing start to the day.

HOW TO WELCOME
NEW BEGINNINGS

However much we might want something new for our lives, when it comes to actually putting it into action, we can often feel overwhelmed by conflicting emotions. We can feel excited about the changes we have decided to make, but also scared when faced with the unknown. We can feel sad about leaving behind what we know, but joyful about the benefits those changes will bring. Although it may feel like you're starting from the beginning again, you aren't. It is a new chapter, another page of your book, and a detour on your journey, but remember that you are still you. You will gain strength and hope in your new beginnings and who knows where they will lead?

Write things down

Make a list of all the positive things you are looking forward to in this new chapter and stick it on your fridge, on your door, or in your calendar so every day you can reinforce what you're looking forward to.

It's OK to feel apprehensive

We are creatures of habit, so it is a completely natural human reaction to feel a bit nervous. But try to acknowledge this feeling and then let it go. Focusing on it will only make it feel bigger and scarier, so go back to thinking about what you're looking forward to instead.

Expect the unexpected

Be excited and embrace anything new that may come your way. Life can be so exciting and new opportunities can come up at any time, so go grab them whenever you can! I know it's a cliché, but it is so true that you really never know what could be around that corner waiting for you. It's exciting!

Be gentle on yourself

We are always our own worst critic. When you're going through life changes and starting new beginnings it's more important than ever to be gentle with yourself. Steer away from thinking about all the things you should have or could have done, as this will just make you fearful. Remember: you're exactly where you need to be right now, so please show yourself some compassion and love.

vitality

Vitality is about going about our day with courage and curiosity. To feel full of vitality, we need to take care of the physical, mental, and emotional aspects of our life, treating each of these with the equal importance they deserve.

Facing each day with vitality will encourage positivity and happiness. By adopting a mindful approach in all that we do, we can embrace our current situation while feeling energized to move forward.

The recipes in this section are bright and colorful and bursting with zingy, happy flavors to wake up your taste buds and make you want to do a little dance!

HOW TO ENCOURAGE
VITALITY IN OUR EVERY DAY

• **Positivity**
Try to adopt a positive attitude. Letting go of negative thought patterns will give you more energy, and make you feel so much happier as you go about your day-to-day activities. We all have to take the trash out and go to work, but don't see these as something negative; it's just part of life.

• **Breathe more**
Breathing feels SO good because it affirms and strengthens the life force that flows through us. Breathing exercises can make you feel more energetic and uplifted as you tune into your breath and allow it to flow more freely (see page 35).

• **Get outside and MOVE**
Try to sneak in some form of movement whenever you can. Go for a walk or a run, do some stretches or whatever you enjoy, but do it daily. Exercise not only will boost your physical strength, but it's also a great stress reliever. Get outside, whatever the weather—it will make you feel alive!

• **Learn new things**
Engaging your brain by learning new things will keep it functioning at its highest level. Don't be afraid to learn a new skill—have the courage to dive headfirst into something you've always wanted to do. Just do it! It will give you life!

• **Sleep**
Your body needs sleep to keep your immune system healthy and to recharge. See pages 32–33 for tips on how to have a more restful night. This is KEY to your overall mental and physical health.

• **Hydrate, hydrate, hydrate!**
Drink at least 6 cups of water daily and opt for herbal teas. Green tea is especially good, as it is also a powerful antioxidant. Drinking water will also help flush out your system, making you feel less sluggish and more energized.

Beautiful Buddha bowls

Buddha bowls are perfect little bowls of nutritionally balanced goodness. This bowl uses quinoa as its base—a brilliant source of protein that releases its energy slowly to keep you going all day. Sweet potatoes are packed with potassium to boost your mood—I love their bright color, too!—and iron-rich kale is great for beating tiredness. Buddha bowls are endlessly versatile, so use whatever ingredients you have; just make sure you have a good balance of protein, veg, and healthy fats. See opposite for some ideas.

For the quinoa and kale

1½ cups quinoa
2½ oz kale, stalks and ribs
  removed, chopped into
  bite-size pieces
½ tsp sea salt
2 tbsp olive oil, plus more to
  drizzle
juice of 1 lime

For the sweet potato

a glug of olive oil
2 small sweet potatoes,
  unpeeled but washed well,
  cut into ¾-inch chunks
2 tsp ground cumin
1 tsp smoked paprika
1½ tsp sea salt

For the tahini dressing

3 tbsp tahini
2 garlic cloves, finely
  chopped
2 green onions, finely
  chopped
juice of 1 lemon
a pinch of sea salt

Extras

1 (15-oz) can chickpeas,
  rinsed and drained
  (you can eat these warm
  or cold)
a handful of sunflower
  seeds and/or chopped nuts
½ avocado, drizzled with
  olive oil
a sprinkle of nigella seeds
a handful of arugula
chopped radish
edible flowers (*optional*)

Cook the quinoa in a saucepan of boiling water for about 15 minutes. Drain and set aside.

Meanwhile, warm some oil in a large frying pan over medium heat. Add the sweet potatoes. Stir in the cumin, paprika, and salt. Once the pan is sizzling, add 3 tablespoons water, cover with a lid, and decrease the heat to low. Cook, stirring occasionally, for about 15 minutes, until the sweet potato is tender. Set aside to cool.

Put the kale in a large bowl. Sprinkle with salt and drizzle with oil. Use your hands to massage the kale for 2 to 3 minutes. Whisk together the 2 tablespoons oil with the lime juice, drizzle over the kale, and toss to coat.

For the tahini dressing, blitz the ingredients in a small blender until smooth.

To serve, mix the quinoa and kale together. Divide between bowls and top each with the sweet potato, chickpeas, and a good spoonful of the tahini dressing. Sprinkle with nuts and seeds and serve with the rest of the extras.

BUILD YOUR OWN BUDDHA BOWL

Here are some suggestions for what to put in your bowl.

PROTEIN: chickpeas, lentils, hummus, tofu, tempeh, black beans, lima beans, nut cheese
GRAINS: quinoa, rice, whole wheat pasta, buckwheat noodles
HEALTHY FATS: an avocado or a tablespoon of pesto, nut butter, or tahini

VEG: roasted sweet potato, spinach, kale, edamame beans, peas, sautéed greens
EXTRAS: herbs, edible flowers, chopped nuts, seeds, dried fruits, plant-based yogurt, dressing

Magic chili

I call this magic chili because it is the ultimate mood-boosting dish, instantly bringing positive vibes to everyone who eats it. Rich in selenium to encourage all those feel-good endorphins, along with beans, which are rich in iron and magnesium to help reduce tiredness, this is my go-to dish for ultimate vitality. The leftovers are good the next day, too, and it will freeze for up to six weeks.

2¼ cups brown rice
2 tbsp olive oil
1 medium onion, chopped
1 garlic clove, crushed
1 tsp ground cumin
1 tsp ground cinnamon
1 tsp ground coriander
1 tsp smoked paprika
1 tsp chile powder
1 cup Brazil nuts, finely
  chopped
1 (15-oz) can kidney beans,
  drained and rinsed
½ (15-oz) can chickpeas,
  drained and rinsed
1 (14.5-oz) can diced
  tomatoes
juice of 2 limes
sea salt and freshly ground
  black pepper

To serve
7 tbsp plant-based plain
  yogurt or crème fraîche
freshly chopped cilantro
1 avocado, sliced
1 fresh chile, chopped

Cook the rice in a saucepan of boiling water for 25 minutes. Drain and set aside.

Meanwhile, heat the oil in a large saucepan and lightly cook the onion and garlic for about 5 minutes, until softened. Stir in the spices and cook for 2 minutes. Add the nuts, beans, chickpeas, tomatoes, lime juice, and ½ cup water. Season with salt and pepper, stir well, and simmer for 20 minutes.

Serve the rice with the chili in bowls, with a spoonful of plant-based yogurt or crème fraîche, plenty of chopped cilantro, and sliced avocado. Sprinkle the chopped fresh chile over the top.

 Use any leftover chili in a breakfast burrito. Or add cooked quinoa and wrap it in a tortilla with salad and chopped tomatoes.

Sweet stuffed spuds

Such an easy lunch or supper dish that can be eaten cold as well as warm, depending on the weather. Sweet potatoes are full of vitamins and antioxidants to keep our immune system strong, which is exactly what we need for our body to renew and revitalize.

For the spuds

1 (15-oz) can chickpeas,
  drained and rinsed
a glug of olive oil
1 tsp chile powder
1 tsp ground cinnamon
1 tsp smoked paprika
sea salt and freshly ground
  black pepper
4 small sweet potatoes,
  unpeeled but washed
  well, halved lengthwise

For the garlic-tahini dressing

3 tbsp tahini
2 garlic cloves, finely
  chopped
2 green onions, finely
  chopped
juice of 1 lemon
a pinch of sea salt

For the tomato topping

⅔ cup cherry tomatoes,
  diced
a small bunch of parsley,
  chopped
a small bunch of cilantro,
  chopped
juice of 1 lemon
½ fresh chile, chopped
⅔ cup toasted almonds,
  roughly chopped

Preheat the oven to 425°F. Line 2 baking sheets with foil.

Spread out the chickpeas on one of the lined baking sheets and toss with olive oil and the spices. Season with salt and pepper. Rub the sweet potatoes with a little oil and place, cut-side down, on the other baking sheet. Place both in the oven and cook for 35 to 45 minutes, until the potatoes are tender and the chickpeas are golden brown.

Meanwhile, make the garlic-tahini dressing by whisking together all the ingredients in a small bowl. Add a little water so that it's pourable. Taste and adjust the seasoning with more salt as needed.

Make the tomato topping by tossing the tomato and herbs with the lemon juice and chile.

Remove the potatoes and chickpeas from the oven. Mash the insides of the potatoes a little, then top with the chickpeas, dressing, tomatoes, and toasted almonds and serve.

 The garlic-tahini dressing will keep in an airtight jar in the fridge for up to 6 weeks. Use it in a sandwich with hummus and salad. Delish.

HOME FRAGRANCE

Running my food business from home and constantly cooking in large quantities means I can be left with lots of odds and ends to use up. Waste is unnecessary and so I try to find weird and wonderful ways to use any leftovers however I can.

I often have lots of gorgeous-smelling lemon and orange peels, as I use the juices for salad dressings and drinks, and so I started making my own homemade air fresheners out of them. It might sound strange, but give it a go and you will never throw away an old lemon rind again! The fresh scent of citrus fruits filling the rooms in my home is so uplifting and energizing.

All you need to do is boil a couple of fruit peels in a pan with about 2 cups water for 20 to 30 minutes, then turn off the heat. It will leave the house smelling divine for hours.

I sometimes also add a stick of cinnamon, a few cloves, or a few sprigs of herbs.

HERE ARE MY FAVORITE COMBINATIONS

- **Orange peel and a cinnamon stick** (and/or a few cloves)—uplifting and a great mood booster. Orange and cinnamon will give your home a cozy, festive aroma.

- **Lemon peel with a sprig of fresh rosemary or thyme**—good for relieving stress. This combination of scents will give your home an almost spa-like serenity! Lemon and rosemary are also good if you have a cold.

- **Grapefruit peel and a 1-inch piece of fresh ginger**—energizing. This stimulating scent will encourage positivity and help restore your get-up-and-go!

TLC

If you are reading this section and are feeling desperately in need of some extra TLC, the first thing I would urge you to do is to give yourself the time and space to recover. Listen to what you need and focus on resting up and getting better. Whatever you have booked in your schedule can wait, and no one will feel upset with you if you have to cancel an appointment because you are unwell or need some time out. Don't feel guilty about needing to give up for a few days. You will not let anyone down.

I know it can be hard, but it's at times like this when tender loving care is exactly what you need, so show yourself some kindness while you heal and get back up to strength.

The recipes in this chapter are packed with nutrient-rich ingredients to build up your physical strength and lift your mood. They will boost serotonin levels and get those happy hormones kicking, which are vital for feeling better. I have also included gut-soothing recipes. There is now thought to be a strong link between our gut health and our mood, so this is something we should all be taking care of, but especially so if we have had to take antibiotics. These comforting, nourishing recipes are also easy to eat and digest, for when your appetite may be lacking.

Stress and illness can have such a negative effect on our body, so one of the very best things you can do for yourself is to make sure you rest and give yourself some much-needed attention. I hope by being kind to yourself, taking time to fully recover, and by eating nutritious wholesome food you'll be back to feeling strong and happy again soon.

GIVE YOURSELF SOME TLC . . .

- **Say no.** You need time to recover properly, so ease up on the commitments for a while.

- **Ask for help.** Don't suffer in silence, feeling like you don't want to bother anyone. Asking for help will take the pressure off, and people will be so happy to give you a hand.

- **Do what you love and what makes you happy.** We are so used to being under constant pressure, we can forget to do what we really enjoy and what gives us pleasure. Get lost in a good book or cook a nourishing meal for yourself (such as the Super Green Nourish Soup on page 176). Make this a priority when you need some extra TLC.

- **Have a digital detox.** Take a break from all things digital. When you're feeling low you can feel vulnerable, so flicking through social media and seeing posts of the perfect lives (which we all know aren't necessarily real) won't do you any good.

- **Pamper yourself.** This doesn't have to mean a trip to the spa—just run a steaming hot bath with your favorite oils (see page 33). Light some candles and play some meditation music while you bathe. There are some impressive links between good mental health and water therapy, so make some time for a proper soak.

- **Be kind to yourself.** What would you say to a friend if they were feeling down? I would imagine you would do everything in your power to give them a boost and try to help them think more positively. So try and practice this on yourself as well. (See the next page for more on how to be kind to yourself.)

BE KIND
TO YOURSELF

Look back over the past week and think about all the people you helped or were kind to. What did you do? What did you say? Write it down.

Were you in that list?

We worry so much about showing kindness to others, but we often forget to be kind to ourselves. There are so many little things you can do to show yourself some kindness. It doesn't have to be a big gesture—just something small will do the job, like making yourself a nourishing lunch to take to work or giving yourself a little time in the morning to stretch and breathe before the crazy rush starts. Or letting yourself off the hook if you've said something or behaved in a way you feel you shouldn't have. Treat yourself with the love and kindness you deserve, the kind of love, kindness, and forgiveness you show others.

Make time for yourself

Every day do something that brings you joy. It doesn't have to take long (because that's not always possible). It might be writing in your journal or sitting at the window and watching the sunset. Or it could be listening to your favorite song all the way through with no interruptions.

Forgive yourself

We've all done stuff we are not proud of, and you know what? It's part of life. Maybe you raised your voice at the kids this morning because they were being naughty and made you all late. Or maybe you can't let go of a missed work opportunity you didn't take. Or it could be something that happened long ago that cuts a bit deeper. Whatever it is, give yourself some slack and forgive yourself because you've learned from that situation and in order to move on you need to be at peace with it.

Be proud of what you've achieved

Go shout it from the rooftops or wear a big grin on your face—it's not showing off. Be proud of your achievements—you worked hard for them. Acknowledge them and enjoy that feeling instead of shying away from it.

Treat yourself

Whether it's a new book or a cheeky afternoon slice of cake with a friend, do it. Make a picnic and go and sit in your favorite spot and take half an hour out of the day. You deserve it, so don't feel guilty.

Believe in YOU

You are amazing. Write it down—or a mantra of your own that you feel connected to—and stick it on your fridge. Write it in your calendar. Write it on your mirror in bright red lipstick! Keep telling yourself you are amazing. You are enough. You are loved. And believe it.

What to eat when you can't face cooking

These simple recipes use just three or four mainly pantry ingredients. They are quick to prepare, with minimum washing up, for when you are feeling completely flat or totally wiped out, and for when cooking really is the last thing on your mind. Especially during these times, we must give our body the nutrition it needs. Low mood and depression can feel empty and cold, so by simply giving yourself something warm to fill you up, you will hopefully start the healing process. Self-care food doesn't have to be a three-course meal, just a dish that gives you some love and makes you feel nurtured inside and out when you need it most.

Toast

• Blend a handful of cashew nuts with a spoonful of nutritional yeast, a splash of water, a clove of garlic, and some fresh parsley. Spread on toast. *Cashews are high in protein, and nutritional yeast is packed with B vitamins, including B_{12}.*

• Mash a can of cannellini beans with chopped garlic and thyme. Mix in a drizzle of olive oil and a squeeze of lemon juice. Spread on toast and finish with a little sea salt. *Cannellini beans are high in protein, as well as containing iron to help you sleep. They are also slow-releasing carbs, for even energy levels.*

Sweet toast

• Almond butter with chopped fruit. *Bananas help boost our happy hormone serotonin, and almond butter provides protein as well as lots of useful vitamins and minerals. Or try any fruit you fancy and have on hand!*

• Make your own fruit jam by crushing a basket of strawberries or raspberries with a fork and mixing with a tablespoon of chia seeds. Leave to set for 15 minutes. Cover and keep in the fridge for up to 1 week. This is a brilliant, healthy alternative to store-bought jams. *Berries are high in antioxidants and vitamin C, and chia seeds are a great source of nutrients such as magnesium and protein. Spread a layer of nut butter on your toast first, for an extra protein boost.*

Baked potatoes

Bake a sweet potato or regular spud and serve with one of these easy toppings:

• Mix a can of drained chickpeas with a tablespoonful each of mango chutney and plant-based plain yogurt and a teaspoon of curry powder. *Chickpeas are high in protein and iron to stabilize energy levels and improve sleep.*

• Mix a couple of tablespoons of hummus with a pinch of sweet smoky paprika and serve with a handful of watercress. *Hummus is full of protein and healthy fats, and the peppery iron-rich watercress will wake up your taste buds.*

Pasta

• Mix together a small handful of chopped walnuts, a spoonful of nutritional yeast and olive oil, and some fresh herbs. Stir into cooked pasta. *Packed with omega-3 and B vitamins.*

• Heat 1½ tbsp olive oil on medium heat and stir in 1 tbsp all-purpose flour for 2 minutes. Add 1 cup plant-based milk, a little at a time, stirring to make a thick sauce. Season with salt and pepper and stir in 1 tbsp nutritional yeast. Boil 3½ oz macaroni in salted water for 8 to 10 minutes. Drain and mix with the sauce, then spoon into a small baking dish and cook in the oven at 400°F for 20 minutes. *Incredibly comforting and indulgent to calm the nerves and help ease anxiety.*

SUPERFOOD SMOOTHIES

When you're feeling tired or unwell, or your mood is low, sometimes it can be hard to rouse the energy to prepare a full meal. That's when smoothies can step in to provide a much-needed easy way of getting in some nutrients. If you don't have all the ingredients in these suggestions, don't worry at all; just throw whatever you have into a blender and blitz until smooth. Play around and find your favorite combinations.

• TLC NOURISHING GREEN

Spirulina is great for energy and is full of nutrients and vitamins. It also contains tryptophan, to boost serotonin production.

1 small banana, sliced
  (it's a good idea to keep
  some sliced bananas in
  the freezer)
1 ripe avocado
a handful of spinach
  and/or kale, stalks
  and ribs removed from
  the kale
1 scoop of spirulina
1 tsp coconut oil
1 tsp honey
2 cups plant-based milk
  of your choice, water, or
  coconut water
1 tbsp chia seeds

• MOOD-BOOSTING SEA-SALTED CACAO

Cacao can really lift your mood, as it helps stimulate the brain to produce feel-good hormones.

½ cup almonds (soaked
  in water for 30 minutes,
  then rinsed under
  running water)
1 cup water
2 pitted dates
1 small banana, sliced
1 tsp nut butter
1 tsp chia seeds
1 tbsp cacao powder
a large pinch of sea salt

• TUMMY-LOVING ENERGIZER

Digestive issues can be closely linked to stress. The apple cider vinegar and ginger will help settle a nervous tummy.

mounded ½ cup
  blueberries
¾-inch piece of fresh
  ginger, peeled
1 tsp ground turmeric
zest and juice of 1 orange
1 tbsp raw apple cider
  vinegar
1 tbsp coconut oil
a pinch of freshly ground
  black pepper
1 cup almond milk (or
  plant-based milk of your
  choice)

Gut-healing broth

The gut plays a vital role in our health by helping control digestion and assisting our immune system. There is also a lot of recent research showing that our gut health has a direct link to our emotions and mood. To help support the growth of healthy bacteria, we need to eat a wide variety of fruits, vegetables, whole grains, and fermented foods. If you have been on medication—especially antibiotics—this broth is a great healer. Freeze in batches so you always have some on hand; it will keep for up to three months.

1 small onion, quartered
1 garlic head, smashed
1 fresh chile, chopped
2-inch piece of fresh ginger, peeled and chopped
3½ cups greens (such as kale)
2 large carrots
2 sticks of celery
1¾ oz dried mushrooms (*optional*)
1¾ oz dried seaweed (*optional*)
1 tbsp coconut or olive oil
1 tbsp peppercorns
2 tbsp ground turmeric
1 tbsp tamari
1 tbsp raw apple cider vinegar
1 tbsp miso paste
a bunch of cilantro, chopped
2 tbsp nutritional yeast (*optional*)
a bunch of parsley, chopped

Put everything, except the parsley, in a large pot with 6 cups water. Bring to a boil, then decrease the heat and simmer, with the lid on, for about 1 hour.

Strain the liquid into a large bowl. Serve immediately with some fresh parsley, or cool and store for later.

You can add noodles or raw veggies to this, or just drink it plain.

Spiced sautéed greens

This is a simple and quick dish to have on its own or as a side. It is packed with iron and folate to increase your energy levels, and the spices will give a boost to your immune system. Add more spices if you like, and any greens you have in the fridge.

1 tbsp coconut oil
3 garlic cloves, minced
2-inch piece of fresh ginger, peeled and chopped
2-inch piece of fresh turmeric, peeled and chopped
9 oz kale, spinach, or chard, or combination of all three, thinly sliced (stalks and ribs removed from the kale)
a pinch of sea salt

Heat the oil in a large saucepan over medium heat. Add the garlic, ginger, and turmeric and cook for 30 seconds. Add the greens, season with salt, and cook for 1 minute. Add 2 tablespoons water to the pan and cook, stirring, until the greens are just wilted, then serve.

 Add some noodles and tofu for a more substantial main dish.

Super green nourish soup

This soup is full of goodness and the creamy coconut milk gives it a really comforting consistency, like someone is giving you a great big hug. Veggies like spinach, kale, and watercress contain high levels of calcium, iron, folate, and vitamins K and A. This magic combination will help reduce tiredness and aid restful sleep, so if you are feeling totally exhausted or wiped out, this soup will really help you recharge.

a glug of olive oil or 1 tsp coconut oil
1 leek, sliced
2 potatoes, chopped
sea salt and freshly ground black pepper
1 tsp freshly grated nutmeg
1 tbsp tamari
5 cups spinach
5¼ oz kale, stalks and ribs removed
3 cups watercress
1 quart veggie stock (see page 18 for homemade)
1 (13.5 oz) can coconut milk
a swirl of plant-based yogurt
chile flakes, sunflower seeds, and edible flowers, to garnish (*optional*)
bread, to serve

Heat the oil in a large saucepan and cook the leek on low heat for a few minutes, until soft.

Add the potatoes, season with salt and pepper, and stir in the nutmeg and tamari. Cook for 5 minutes.

Add the spinach, kale, and watercress and put the lid on. Leave on low heat for 5 minutes, then pour in the stock and cook for 15 minutes, until the potato is soft.

Add the coconut milk and, using a handheld blender, blitz until smooth (or blend in a countertop blender). Add more water if you like a thinner consistency. Warm through for a few minutes, then serve with a swirl of plant-based yogurt, chile flakes, sunflower seeds, and edible flowers, if desired.

 Add some chopped fresh chile and cayenne pepper if you'd like a bit of heat.

Hearty stew with sweet potato mash

When we are feeling poorly or run down, sometimes we just want comforting foods that are easy to eat. The seaweed in this stew is a rich source of several minerals, including calcium, magnesium, potassium, copper, and iron, which we need to boost our energy and lift our mood. If you can't find it, though, don't worry; the other ingredients are perfectly balanced for optimum nutritional health. This stew is very hearty and filling, so a small portion will go a long way—keep the rest in the fridge or freezer for later.

a glug of olive oil
½ small onion, chopped
4 garlic cloves, finely
  chopped
3 carrots, chopped
1 small red bell pepper,
  chopped
2 celery sticks, chopped
7 oz mushrooms, sliced
sea salt
3 cups veggie stock (see
  page 18 for homemade)
¾ cup dried red lentils
a sprig of fresh thyme,
  leaves picked (or 1 tsp
  dried thyme)
1 tsp dried sage
1 bay leaf
2 tsp tomato paste
a handful of dried seaweed,
  such as wakame
  (*optional*)
1 tbsp raw apple cider
  vinegar
1 tbsp tamari
1 (15-oz) can lima beans,
  drained
3⅓ cups spinach, chopped
freshly chopped parsley

**For the sweet potato
mash**

3 medium sweet potatoes,
  chopped
sea salt and freshly ground
  black pepper
2 tbsp olive oil
a small bunch of chives,
  chopped (*optional*)

Heat some olive oil on medium heat in a large saucepan.
Add the onion and garlic and cook for 1 minute. Add the
carrots, red bell pepper, celery, mushrooms, and a good
pinch of salt and cook for 5 minutes.

Add the stock, lentils, herbs, tomato paste, seaweed if
using, vinegar, and tamari and give it a good stir. Cook
for about 20 minutes on low heat, until the lentils are
cooked through. Then add the lima beans.

While the stew is cooking, cook the sweet potatoes in
a large saucepan of boiling water for about 20 minutes
until tender, and drain. Mash the potatoes with a fork or
potato masher, adding the 2 tbsp oil and seasoning with
salt and pepper as desired. Add some chopped chives for
extra flavor, if you like.

Stir the spinach into the stew and serve with a dollop of
the mash. Garnish with fresh parsley.

 *Try mashed celery root instead of sweet potato—or a
mixture of potato and parsnip.*

Nourishing crumble

I have been making veggie crumble since I was a kid and it has to be one of the most comforting meals ever—root veggies in a creamy sauce with a tasty oaty topping. It's full of goodness and a real treat to eat. This will keep for three days in the fridge or six weeks in the freezer, so save leftovers for when you don't feel like cooking. Simply defrost and reheat in the oven at 350°F for 20 to 25 minutes.

For the veggies

a glug of olive oil
1 small onion, chopped
2 garlic cloves, finely sliced
7 oz celery root (about ½
  small one), peeled and
  diced
2 parsnips, peeled and
  diced
9 oz sweet potatoes, diced
1¼ cups veggie stock (see
  page 18 for homemade)
1¾ cups plant-based plain
  yogurt
2 large tomatoes, chopped
1 to 2 tsp miso paste
a pinch of freshly grated
  nutmeg
1 tsp dried oregano
a small bunch of parsley,
  chopped
salt and freshly ground
  black pepper

For the topping

1½ cups rolled oats
¾ cup plus 2 tbsp
  whole wheat flour
6 tbsp coconut oil, softened
sea salt
1 tbsp sesame seeds
1 tbsp sunflower seeds
a handful of Brazil nuts,
  roughly chopped
2 tbsp nutritional yeast

Preheat the oven to 400°F. Heat some olive oil in a large saucepan over medium heat and gently cook the onion and garlic for 5 minutes. Add all the root veggies and the stock, bring to a boil, and reduce the heat to low and simmer for about 15 minutes, until the veggies are soft.

Meanwhile, to make the crumble, place the oats, flour, coconut oil, and a pinch of salt in a large bowl. Rub together with your fingertips until the mixture resembles very coarse breadcrumbs. Add a tablespoon more oil if it seems too dry. Add the remaining crumble ingredients and set aside.

When the veg is soft, stir in the plant-based yogurt, chopped tomatoes, 1 teaspoon of the miso, the nutmeg, and the herbs and season with pepper. Taste and adjust the seasoning, adding more miso if necessary. Spoon the mixture into a 9 × 13-inch baking dish and spread the crumble mixture on top.

Bake for 35 minutes, until the crumble is golden. Place a sheet of foil over the top if it's browning too quickly.

Add some chopped fresh chile and cayenne pepper if you'd like a bit of heat.

Dreamy brownies

When you're feeling a bit low, something sweet can be a real cure-all. These brownies are so delicious, you will not believe they are such a healthy snack. They will give you all the TLC you need, as cacao is full of minerals and vitamins to boost your mood and energy levels, dates are a wonderful natural sweetener, and the nuts add protein. These also make a great gift for a friend who might be feeling under the weather.

For the brownies
1½ cups pecans or walnuts
generous ¾ cup dried
  pitted dates, soaked in
  hot water for 10 minutes
6 tbsp cacao powder
5 tbsp shredded coconut
3 tbsp honey or maple
  syrup
a pinch of sea salt

For the frosting
generous ¾ cup dried
  pitted dates, soaked in hot
  water for 10 minutes (save
  the water after soaking)
¼ cup cacao powder
2 tbsp coconut oil

Optional toppings
chopped walnuts and
  slivered almonds
freeze-dried raspberries
edible rose petals

Blitz the nuts in a food processor until crumbly. Add the dates and blitz again until the mixture sticks together. Add the remaining ingredients and blend until the mixture turns a lovely dark brown. (If you don't have a food processor, chop the nuts and dates finely and combine with the rest of the ingredients to make a fairly firm brownie mixture.)

Line an 8-inch square cake pan with parchment paper and spoon the mixture into it, pressing down firmly.

To make the frosting, put all the ingredients in a food processor or blender with 3 tablespoons of the reserved date-soaking liquid and blitz for a few minutes until smooth and velvety. Add a little more water if the mixture seems dry. Using a spatula, spread the frosting on top of the brownie mixture. Sprinkle with any toppings you are using, and chill for 1 hour in the fridge before serving.

I usually slice the brownies before putting them in the fridge to chill as they are easier to cut before they have been chilled.

IT'S OK TO NOT BE OK

It can often feel like society expects us to be happy and positive all the time and that we should all thrive on being busy. This can leave us feeling under so much pressure, as though showing any kind of sadness or letting people know that we need to take a step back for a while to recharge is a sign of weakness.

Our energy levels naturally ebb and flow throughout our lives, and we all know that life isn't perfect—sometimes it feels like a great big rollercoaster! Just as you will have days when everything feels great, there will be times when it feels the complete opposite. And that's OK. That's what life is like. We can't be like Mary Poppins all the time!

It's so important not to compare your life or yourself with others. I know this is easier said than done, especially within the world of social media, but when you're not feeling your best it can be a dangerous thing to do.

If you speak up and stop saying everything is OK when it isn't, you are encouraging a more honest and meaningful relationship with yourself and those around you. Remember that the people who care about you have your best interests at heart. They will want to help you in any way they can. Think how you would feel if a friend was going through a tough time but felt they couldn't open up to you. You are not a bother to others; and by telling someone you are not OK you won't be adding to their own problems. Please remember that. Speak up and reach out when you don't feel OK. When you do ask for help or tell someone how you are feeling, it can make things feel a little bit easier and lighten that heavy load you've been carrying around.

Talking about how we really feel and saying "I'm not OK" is a sign of strength. By bringing it up in our conversations we're taking the first step toward asking for help when we need it most, and it will encourage others to ask for help if they need it, too.

Index

Page references in *italics* indicate images.

About Gem

Gem grew up in a large family, and as the youngest child of five is used to being surrounded by lots of noise and happy chaos! She learned to cook from her mum, who is not only a fantastic cook but also taught her how to cook on a budget. Batch cooking and being smart with ingredients are ideas Gem follows daily. Gem would often cook for the whole family from as young as eight years old, and this is where her passion for cooking started.

During her teenage years, Gem suffered from anorexia, but luckily she recovered, thanks to the love and support of her family. Most of her twenties were spent partying, and in her early thirties, Gem experienced a number of miscarriages. Through these experiences, she worked out the link between eating well and feeling better, both physically and mentally. She started eating more plant-based foods and focused on eating for physical health as well as continuing to experiment with mood foods. And it worked!

Being blessed with two healthy children was a real turning point for Gem. After she had been working in the mental health sector as a drug counselor for many years, the family decided to go to Barcelona for an adventure—and ended up staying for two and a half years! While there, Gem set up a vegan takeout business from their central apartment, often preparing vegan bento box picnics for traveling DJs, as they were all sick of airline food! Word spread and Gem's business was doing very well. They moved back to Brighton, where Gem's Wholesome Kitchen was born. Gem and her husband run it together now—Gem does the cooking and Peter looks after the business.

Gem loves cooking up a feast to share with family and friends that tastes good, provides energy, is mood-boosting, and makes everyone happy. Like her food, she is bright, colorful, full of love, and FUN!

Thank you

Thank you to Sam and Emma and all the others at Penguin Random House for giving me the opportunity to create my first book. I still can't believe it.

Thank you to Laura Herring, my editor, for being so supportive throughout this process and making my words sound so good.

Thank you to Nikki for designing the book so beautifully and being so helpful, so supportive, and so much fun on photoshoot days.

Thank you to James Bellorini for shooting the UK front cover so beautifully and for the portraits of me inside that capture me so well.

Thanks to Mark at Potters Thumb in Brighton and Carolina Blue in Barcelona for letting me use the beautiful handmade pottery for so many of the shots in this book.

Thank you to Matt Inwood, who inspired me greatly with my photography and helped me so much at the beginning of my journey.

Thank you to all my friends and family who have supported me this year while I have been writing this book. Especially my mum, who taught me to cook and love food from an early age.

Thank you to all my wonderful clients in Brighton, who continue to support Gem's Wholesome Kitchen and eat my food!

Most important, thank you to my husband, Peter, and my children, Carmen and Hendrix, who have been my rock throughout this process and never complained when I had to work long hours to get everything done. Especially to Peter, who helped manage the business and kids when my head was stuck in the computer for days! I love you all so much.

This book is for YOU.